I0054071

Options Trading
for Beginners

*Everything You Need to Know to
Build Your Portfolio*

TABLE OF CONTENTS

INTRODUCTION

Welcome to the exciting world of professional options trading! Options Trading: A Beginner's Guide to Highly Profitable Option Trades - Proven Strategies, Trading Tools, Rules, and Money Management provides a comprehensive overview of the investment world and a detailed insider's view of what options trading is and how you can benefit from developing your expertise in this area.

In the modern workplace, independence, autonomy, and initiative have been transformed from job skills that can set you apart from the crowd into necessary skills we all need to survive and thrive in the modern professional workplace. Traditionally, the main concerns of every employee were contained entirely within his or her job description. Constant, rapid changes spurred by the growth of the information technology industry have resulted in decentralized workplaces in which we are empowered with the tools and resources to look after our own interests.

If you're like most people, you're accustomed to a human resources department that employs financial experts who are paid to ensure your retirement and savings plans are professionally managed. As the responsibility for managing retirement savings shifts more and more onto the individual employee, learning about the financial tools available to you has become increasingly important.

We are glad you have taken steps to increase your financial literacy by reading *Options Trading*. This book will provide guidance and detailed information about how to increase the value and security of your investment portfolio. Features include:

- A glossary of financial terms
- An overview of the different types of investments
- A detailed analysis of how options contracts work
- Several examples of different options trading strategies
- Do's and don'ts of the options trade

Again, congratulations on your decision to pursue the exciting opportunities awaiting you as a professional options trader!

1

GLOSSARY OF TERMS

By reading this document, the reader agrees that under no circumstances is the author responsible for any losses, direct or indirect, which are incurred as a result of the use of information contained within this document, including but not limited to, errors, omissions, or inaccuracies.

Investment Terminology for the Options Trader

Options traders occupy a privileged niche in the world of investing. The options trader uses a combination of knowledge, training, experience, and expertise to enhance his or her ability to find ways to make the stock market a place where his or her time and effort is repaid. Knowledge of the options trade provides an avenue by which any investor can not only transform his or her existing financial portfolio into a more fully developed, diversified, and higher-paying collection of assets, but also learn to generate additional income completely independent of more traditional investment in underlying securities, such as stocks, bonds, and commodities.

Yes, options trading does require some knowledge of how the markets work, but with the right preparation and a diligent and disciplined approach, any skilled investor can make options trading lively, interesting, exciting, and rewarding. Perhaps more than any other area of investing, professional options traders have developed a language unique to their niche of investing. This book is written for the beginning options trader, so we have used language that is plain and straightforward wherever possible. Of course, part of the fun of options trading is learning to speak this new language. This chapter consists of a glossary of terms used in this book. Many of the terms are relevant throughout the entire investment world; many others are specific to options trading; most of them receive more in-depth treatment, including specific examples and illustrations, in corresponding chapters of this book. This glossary is intended as an easy and convenient reference to help you gain mastery as a professional options trader. The list of terms in this glossary is neither exhaustive nor absolute, and we encourage you to continue building your own glossary alongside ours, especially when you encounter any new additions to the already vibrant vocabulary of today's professional options trader.

Asset: an asset is an economic resource owned by a company or individual. The opposite of an asset is a liability. Different types of assets include

current assets, such as cash, accounts receivable, and inventory; **fixed assets**, such as buildings and equipment; **financial assets**, such as stocks and bonds; and **intangible assets**, such as trademarks and patents.

Assignment: an assignment is a notice received by the holder of an option contract that requires the holder to either sell (for a put option) or buy (for a call option) the underlying assets represented in the contract.

At-the-money (ATM): a term used to describe the relationship between the strike price in an options contract and the current trading price of the shares of the underlying asset. When the strike price is the same as the current market value, the option is at-the-money.

Automatic exercise value: the value of the underlying asset of a capped style options contract at a time of day specified by the options market in which the option is being traded. The term is used only in reference to capped options.

Bear: a bear market is characterized by an overall decline in the value of stocks; investors who are "bearish" on a given stock expect the stock to decline in value and will look for a way to profit from this declining value.

Bond: a type of very large loan issued to governments or corporations for large infrastructure or expansion projects. Individuals investors may act as the lender by purchasing a bond for a portion of the total amount borrowed. The bond contains the terms of the loan repayment, and the bondholder receives repayment of the principal plus interest.

Bull: a bull market is characterized by a general increase in the value of stocks; investors who are "bullish" on a given stock expect the stock to increase in value and will look for a way to profit from this increasing value.

Buy: one of two possible actions an options trader can take to open a transaction. An options trader can buy either a "put" option or a "call" option. The other possible opening action is to sell.

Call: an options trading term that means to buy the underlying assets of an options contract. For example, if an investor buys a call option contract that controls 100 shares of stock, that call option gives him the right to buy the 100 shares.

Cap interval: a constant value established by the options market, which, when combined with the strike price, determines the cap price of the option. The term is used only in reference to capped options.

Cap price: the value that the **automatic exercise value** must reach for the option to be automatically exercised. The term is used only in reference to capped options.

Capped option: a capped option is one of 3 styles of options contract. Capped options are automatically exercised before they expire if the option reaches the automatic exercise value. The other two styles are American style options and European style options.

Cash-settled option: one of two types of options. Cash-settled options give the options holder the right to receive a cash payment for the difference between the value of the underlying asset and the strike price of the options contract. The other type of option is a **physical delivery option**.

Cash settlement amount: the amount of cash the holder of a cash-settled options contract is entitled to receive at the time the options contract is exercised.

Closing transaction: one of several transactions taken by an options trader to exit an options contract. A trader who holds a call option can close the transaction by selling the options contract. A trader who has sold an options contract can close the transaction by buying the same options contract.

Collateralized debt obligation (CDO): a type of derivative investment that repackages "debt obligations," such as mortgages or student loans, then resells them to investors who earn profit based on the value of interest repayments.

Commodity: a type of asset that includes agricultural products, energy-related products, and precious metals.

Contract size: the number of shares represented by an options contract. Normally, one options contract represents 100 shares of an underlying asset.

Covered option: an options contract in which the holder or seller of the options contract owns the underlying shares represented in the contract.

Delivery: a term used to describe the transfer of ownership of shares when a physical delivery options contract is exercised.

Delta: the amount of change in value of an options contract in relation to the change in value of the underlying stock.

Derivative: a type of investment whose value is "derived" from an asset, not tied directly to that asset. Options contracts are derivatives because their value is derived from the value of the underlying stock. Stocks have real value tied to the company in which they represent an interest.

Exchange-traded fund: a type of mutual fund in which the assets in the fund are bought and sold continually throughout each trading day.

Exercise: a term used to describe the action of an options trader when they either buy or sell the underlying stock in a physical delivery options contract or receive the cash settlement amount of a cash-settled options contract.

Exercise settlement value: the difference between the strike price of a cash-settled option and the market value of the underlying stock at the time the option is exercised.

Expiration date: the date on which the options contract expires. An options contract must either be exercised prior to this date, or it expires worthless.

Equity: the amount of money invested in a company by shareholders

Equity option: an options contract that gives the holder the right to buy or sell 100 shares of stock.

Future: a type of derivative investment used to help traders who buy and sell commodities protect against volatility in the market.

Historical volatility: the measured volatility of a specific stock over a specific period of time.

Holder: an options trader who has bought an options contract. A trader can hold either a put option or a call option.

Implied volatility: one of six factors used to determine the price—or premium—of an options contract. Implied volatility is a measure of projected future changes in the value of a given stock; the higher the level of implied volatility, the more expensive the premium to purchase the options contract.

In-the-money (ITM): a term used to describe a profitable options contract. A call option is "in-the-money" if the strike price is below the market value of the underlying stock; a put option is "in-the-money" if the strike price is above the market value of the underlying stock.

Internationally traded options: options that are traded between two markets, each in a different country.

Intrinsic value: the amount by which an options contract is in-the-money.

Index fund: a mutual fund in which the stocks and bonds that comprise the fund are chosen and managed specifically so that their performance will mirror a particular segment of the market.

Index option: options contracts that derive their value from projected changes in the value of a given market index, rather than from any specific stocks.

Long: a term to describe ownership of an asset. An investor who purchases stock is considered to be "long" on that stock.

Market participants: the four parties involved in any given options trade: a buyer of call options; the seller of call options; the buyer of put options; and the seller of put options.

Married option: an option that is purchased at the same time as the underlying stock.

Multiply traded options: options that are traded in two different options markets, both of which are in the same country.

Mutual fund: a type of investment in which many investors pool their contributions into a single fund, which is used to purchase a selection of stock and bonds. If you have a 401(k) or an IRA, you are probably invested in a mutual fund.

Naked option: also called an uncovered option, an options contract that is purchased by an investor who does not own any of the underlying stock.

Opening transaction: the sale or purchase of an options contract that initiates an options trade.

Options quote: an options quote is generated when an options trader buys or sells an options contract. Options quotes follow a specific format. For example, a call option to buy 100 shares of Company ABC stock at $50 at the end of July would read, "ABC July 50 Call." A put option for the same stock would read, "ABC July 50 Put."

Out-of-the-money (OTM): a term used to describe the relationship between the strike price of an option contract and the market value of the underlying stock when there is no financial benefit to the owner of the options contract.

Physical delivery option: one of two types of options contracts. Physical delivery options give the options holder the right to receive or transfer ownership of the underlying interest in an options contract. The other type of option is a **cash-settled option**.

Put: an options trading term that means to sell the underlying assets of an options contract. For example, if an investor buys a put option contract that controls 100 shares of stock, that put option gives him the right to sell the 100 shares.

Premium: the cost of an options contract. There are many factors used to determine the premium, including the value of the underlying stock, market volatility, and whether the option is in-the-money, at-the-money, or out-of-the-money.

Profit-and-Loss graph: a graphic representation of possible outcomes of an options trading strategy.

Risk: the degree to which an investment strategy may differ from the expected result.

Security: an asset that can be traded on the open market.

Sell: one of two possible actions an options trader can take to open a transaction. An options trader can sell either a "put" option or a "call" option. The other possible opening action is to buy.

Short: a term that describes selling an asset. It is possible for an options trader to sell stocks he or she does not own.

Spread: a range of values created by buying several options contracts on the same underlying stock. Depending on the type of spread, the options contracts will have either different strike prices, different expiration dates, or a combination of both.

Standard deviation: in options trading, this term describes the normal change in value of a stock over time. Stocks that have a high standard deviation carry greater risk, but also potentially higher returns.

Strike price: the pre-agreed price in an options contract at which the parties to the contract may either buy or sell the underlying share of stock.

Stock: a security that represents ownership in a company. All of the individual shares of a company together represent the total stock of that company.

Stock symbol: the identifier used by a publicly-traded company for trading purposes. For example, the stock symbol of Microsoft Corporation is MSFT, and this is how the company would be identified in an options quote.

Stock options: a contract that gives the owner of the contract the right to buy or sell 100 shares of the stock named in the contract, according to pre-agreed terms.

Swap: a type of derivative investment in which investors change terms of financial arrangements, such as interest rates or currency exchange rates.

Theta: the amount of change in value of an options contract in relation to its proximity to the expiration date.

Time value: value that is added to intrinsic value to determine the total value of an options contract. The closer an option is to its expiration date, the less time value it has.

Tolerance: the amount of risk an investor is willing to take in any given investment.

Uncovered option: also called a **naked option**, an option contract in which the investor does not own any of the underlying shares.

Underlying asset: the stock, commodity, or other security upon which an options contract is written.

Vega: the amount the value of an options contract will change in relation to the option contract's Implied Volatility.

Vertical spread: one of 3 types of spreads. A vertical spread is created by buying several options contracts on the same underlying stock, each with different strike prices. The other 2 types of spread are horizontal spread and diagonal spreads.

Wings: in a **vertical spread**, the highest and lowest strike prices.

Write: to sell an options contract, an investor can write either a put option or a call option.

Writer: an investor who has sold an options contract that is still open (has not been exercised). Options writers must tolerate more risk that options buyers; writing puts and uncovered calls involves substantial risk.

2

INVESTMENT BASICS

This book is written for the beginning options trader. While options trading generally requires some experience and background in investing, every beginning options trader may benefit from a general review of the major parts of the global financial trade, and where options trading fits in.

Many people are intimidated by the idea of trading on the stock market and often regard the entire financial trade as a hopelessly chaotic and impossibly complex mix of exotic terms, difficult-to-grasp legal concepts, and inaccessible financial terminology. Fortunately, this book's main focus is the practice of options trading. As a result, its discussion of related investment terminology will be to place options trading in its context among the many types of investments that make the stock market such an exciting place.

Types of Investments

Securities

When most people think about the stock market, they think about stocks and bonds. Taken together, though the precise definition may vary depending on the context or location, a security is essentially any type of asset that can be traded on the open market. There are three main types of securities--equity securities, debt securities, and hybrid securities.

Stocks

Stocks are a form of equity security. A company may issue shares of its stock--either common stock or private stock--to investors. Investors who purchase "stock" in a company assume part ownership of the company. When the company's performance results in increased profits, the price of each individual share of its stock rises. Shareholders may receive dividends--or annual payouts--when the value of a company's stock increases over the course of a year.

Bonds

Bonds are a form of debt security. Purchasing a bond gives you interest in a sum of money that was borrowed and must be repaid. By purchasing a bond, you contribute to the funding for the money that has been borrowed. In addition, when bonds are issued there is generally a specified repayment date (maturity date) and interest rate. Bond purchasers are entitled to repayment of principal and interest during this time. Some common types of bonds include Certificates of Deposit (CDs) and government bonds.

Hybrid Securities

Hybrid securities combine aspects of equity securities and debt securities. Equity warrants are a type of options contract. (We will discuss options in more detail later.) Convertible bonds are bonds that may be converted to stock in the issuing company. Preferred stock in a company provides guaranteed repayment terms similar to bonds. All of these types of securities are hybrid securities.

Mutual Funds

Mutual funds are a type of investment commonly referred to as "pooled investments." With a mutual fund, many people invest in, or "pool," their money into a single "fund," which is usually comprised of a variety of different stocks, bonds, and other securities. Those who invest in the mutual fund each receive a share of the money earned from their investment, proportionate to the amount they contribute. If you have a 401(k) or an Individual Retirement Account (IRA) with your employer, your monthly contributions are probably invested in a mutual fund.

Index Funds

An index fund is a specific type of mutual fund. With mutual funds, the fund manager will likely evaluate each of the individual stocks and bonds--the securities--that make up the fund to ensure they continue to provide a good return on investment. Index funds are managed differently--rather than evaluating the performance of each individual security in the fund, the fund manager will evaluate the entire portfolio, modeling it after a segment of the stock market itself (an index), so that the fund's performance as a whole will reflect the performance of the market.

Exchange-Traded Funds (ETFs)

Exchange-traded funds (ETFs) are another type of mutual fund. There is one fundamental difference between ETFs and traditional mutual funds. Traditional mutual funds trade just once a day. Trading begins when the market opens, and the trading on that fund concludes when the market closes. This once-per-day trading determines the daily profits or losses for the fund. By contrast, ETFs are traded continuously throughout each day, so the value of the ETF and of all its underlying securities can fluctuate throughout the day.

Derivatives

Derivatives are also a type of security, but they differ in nature from the types of securities discussed thus far. The value of stocks, bonds, and mutual funds are based on the value of the actual assets themselves. For example, if you own stock in a computer software company, the value of that stock is tied directly to the value of the software as it is sold to distributors and merchants. Generally speaking, when there is increased demand for the software product in the market, the value of the software increases, and so does the value of each of the shares of stock in the company.

Derivatives are different because the value of a derivative is not tied directly to the value of the asset for which the investor has purchased shares. As their name implies, the value of derivatives is **derived** from the value of an asset, rather than tied directly to the value of an asset.

For example, let's imagine a venture capitalist in Asia wanted to invest in an American computer software company. At the time of the sale, the Asian investor has a portfolio made up of assets entirely in Asian currency. He invests in the American company by making a purchase through a U.S. broker using U.S. currency. Although he has made a sound investment, he is concerned that if the value of his Asian currency increases, the overall value of his portfolio will decrease, since it is now comprised of a sizeable amount of shares in U.S. currency. This risk is called exchange-rate risk, and often international investors will compensate for potential losses by purchasing a **currency derivative**.

A currency derivative is a security based on the value of exchange rates. Because the value of these types of securities are based on exchange rates and because they only derive their value from the underlying assets--the international currencies themselves--they are referred to as derivatives. This derivative, in particular, works like an insurance policy by allowing the investor to trade international securities at a guaranteed exchange rate.

There are many types of derivatives. The following are some of the most common:

Collateralized Debt Obligations (CDOs)

CDOs are a complex area of investment. Essentially, a CDO derives its value from an underlying pool of assets that are comprised of debt obligations, including home mortgages, student loans, and bonds. The debt obligations are "collateralized" by securities firms. The repackaged loans and debt obligations are then sold to investors.

Swaps

Swaps are a type of derivative often used to allow investors to exchange--or "swap"--the terms of money management within a financial agreement. Common types of swaps include interest rate swaps and exchange rate swaps.

Futures

Futures contracts--or futures--are sales agreements between investors that specify the sale, purchase, and delivery of a specified commodity at an agreed price and an agreed date in the future. Futures are traded on the stock exchange. Futures contracts are used to hedge against losses caused by volatility in the market. Futures contracts are also used as financial tools by speculators who want to profit from changes in the market if they believe they can predict whether certain commodities will gain or lose value in the future.

Forwards

Forwards are very similar to futures. However, forwards are "over-the-counter" investment products and are not traded on the stock exchange. As a result, forward contracts carry greater risk because the likelihood that either the buyer or seller will not be able to fulfill his obligation in the contract is greater, and there is less opportunity to mitigate losses by trading or selling the agreement on the exchange.

Options

Options contracts--the subject of this book--are very similar to futures contracts. Options contracts are structured as agreements to buy and/or sell a given asset at a specified date in the future at a previously agreed-upon price. The essential difference between a futures contract and an options contract is that futures contracts are structured so that the intent is to complete the purchase or sale. With an options contract, there is no obligation for either party to complete the sale or purchase upon which the contract is based. Options contracts are designed as financial tools to help investors hedge against losses in the event of changes in market conditions, or to profit based on their ability to speculate how prices will fluctuate.

Hard Assets

Thus far, we have looked at securities, which are assets such as stocks and bonds whose value is tied directly to the goods and/or services produced by the companies in whom the investor owns an interest. We have also examined derivatives, which are assets whose value is derived from the value of underlying securities and how that value may be affected by changes in the market.

Hard assets are physical, tangible materials. Some hard assets are traded as raw resources; others are end-used products for businesses and individual consumers. Derivatives such as futures and options derive their value from the purchase and sale not only of securities interests in companies but also of hard assets.

Commodities

The commodities that are commonly traded on the stock market are grouped into categories:

- Metals:
  - □ gold
  - □ silver
  - □ platinum
  - □ copper

- Energy:
  - □ crude oil
  - □ heating oil
  - □ gasoline
  - □ natural gas

- Livestock:
  - □ lean hogs
  - □ pork bellies
  - □ live cattle
  - □ feeder cattle

- Agriculture:
  - □ corn
  - □ soybeans
  - □ wheat
  - □ rice
  - □ cocoa
  - □ coffee
  - □ cotton
  - □ sugar

Other investments

Many investors who have found the stock market a profitable place for building wealth often reinvest their returns in hard assets that may not be traded on the market. These investments may allow for reinvestments in assets the can protect wealth or create residual income streams.

- Real estate:
  - □ residential homes
  - □ land
  - □ commercial buildings
  - □ multifamily structures

- Valuables:
  - □ classic cars
  - □ antiques

3

MONEY AND RISK MANAGEMENT

So far, this book has provided a glossary of investment terminology commonly used among investors. Chapter 2 provided a much more narrow and focused view of some of these terms, with the goal of helping you understand where options trading sits in relation to much of the day-to-day activity that comprises trading and investment in the stock market. Hopefully by now, you have begun to get your bearings. But before we dive into an in-depth exploration of options trading and the strategies that can be used to make these investment tools work for you, let's take some time to consider some of the foundational concepts of smart investing and money management.

Is the Stock Market Right for Me?

Most employers at one time or another have offered their employees a retirement and savings benefits package. Most people who work for such employers enroll in these programs and can enjoy significant financial benefits as they near retirement. If you have some type of employer-sponsored retirement savings account--whether it's a 401(k), an IRA, or some related savings account--then you are already investing in the stock market. These accounts are generally comprised of mutual funds and other securities. Professional fund managers monitor the performance of the securities in these portfolios with the goal of ensuring that the monthly contributions deducted from your paycheck attain the highest return on investment (ROI) possible.

Again, if you are like most people, even though your enrollment in your employer-sponsored retirement savings account qualifies you as a stock market investor, you may not be actively involved in making investment decisions. To be fair, most of us don't like to think about retirement. What's more, investing in the stock market successfully requires knowledge, skill, time, and effort. Because options trading requires some advanced knowledge of basic trading and investment, taking a little time to review your financial, professional, and personal goals is an important first step to ensuring your efforts in options trading bring you the results you want.

Getting Started

Before you determine how to open your first options trading account, taking a snapshot of your current financial resume and mapping out your journey to success is mandatory. All of this preliminary work can seem overwhelming, and often people shy away from investment opportunities because they are intimidated. But if we take the preparatory steps one by one, your initiation into the world of options trading will go much more smoothly.

Savings vs. Investing

In movies and advertisements, investing and life on Wall Street are often portrayed as a romantic and exciting. As in all areas of professional life, there may be some truth to these portrayals. However, investing is not something you should enter into lightly or casually. If you are diligent, knowledgeable, and seek out credible and trustworthy sources of information and support, there is no reason why you cannot become a successful investor, but success requires that you have at least some definite idea about your ultimate financial goals.

Thus, the first question you might like to ask yourself is whether your goal is simply to save money or whether you are serious about becoming an active investor. There is nothing wrong with making monthly contributions to an IRA or a 401(k) account. Many people are able to save a lot of money for retirement this way. But simply saving money is entirely different from investing.

Setting Goals

If you have made the decision to move from saving to active investing, setting goals will become one of the most important tools to ensure your ongoing success. Up until now, if you have been an active saver with an employer-sponsored retirement savings account, you have probably already assembled a fairly impressive toolbox of planning and goal-setting tools. Even if most of your planning and goal-setting has been focused on your professional--or even personal--goals and responsibilities, those very same habits can be adapted to help you establish goal-setting routines that will help you succeed in the world of options trading.

Risk Management

Fear and risk are probably the two biggest reasons many people never take the leap from saving to investing. "What if I lose all my money?" "What if my investments end up earning me less money than my savings and retirement account?" These fears should not be entirely dismissed. But remember that if you are asking these questions, you are already thinking about some of the fundamental basics of investing. Don't let your burgeoning awareness of investing in the stock market prevent you from pursuing your goals. Now that you have considered the difference between merely saving and actively investing, part of your investment plan should most definitely include risk assessment.

As an options trader, you will definitely have to consider risks. In fact, without the constant presence of financial risk, options trading itself would not exist. To succeed as an options trader, it is imperative that you move from a mindset in which you regard risk as an invariably bad thing to a mindset in which you are able to see that risk--when properly managed--will be the key to successful investment.

Options trading can help you mitigate risk--and even profit from risk--in every area of your financial life. For example, if your retirement and savings investments are not producing the kind of wealth you need to retire comfortably, options trading can help you mitigate that risk by providing an additional source of investment income. In addition, if you are already a skilled investor, learning about options trading can help you understand that the inherent risks of the market can help you make money even when the risks don't go your way.

Diversification

Diversification is a term used to indicate that an investment portfolio contains more than just one type of investment. Most investors know that a diversified portfolio will withstand risk better than a portfolio with only one type of investment. If the market declines in one way, having investments in another area can compensate for losses. If the market surges in many areas, you will enjoy greater profit by having investments in all those areas rather than only one.

While diversification works from this general standpoint, diversification can also lead to success in options trading. There are many different types of options contracts, many different opportunities for writing options contracts, and many different strategies that options traders use to benefit from the risks inherent in investing. Your skill as an options trader will increase in proportion to the degree to which you are willing to master as many of these techniques as possible.

Distribution, Taxes, and Re-investment

Once you have completed a financial self-assessment, formulated a basic plan of action, and successfully begun your career as an active investor, you may be tempted to let your guard down, sit back, and wait for the money to roll in. Certainly, a sound investment plan will give you some breathing room and peace of mind, but becoming a skilled investor is really only one side of the complete investment picture.

Once you have established a viable path to financial success through investment, you will be faced with concerns that are similar to those that led down this path to begin with. Specifically, how can you protect the money you have earned as a result of your efforts in investing? How can you ensure that your investment earnings continue to generate a personal source of income for you, much as you were concerned that the salary from your job was earning dividends for your retirement?

You can't just put your investment earnings in a big sack or stuff them in the mattress. The final step of a sound financial investment plan involves understanding how to make your investments continue to work for you by capitalizing on tools in distribution, taxation, and re-investment.

What kind of investor are you?

By now, you should be feeling a little more comfortable about starting your career in options trading. However, to succeed in this area of investing, formulating a well-designed plan and sticking with it will always be the key to success. Be honest with yourself as you consider your current state of financial literacy and skill. It's okay if you're not ready to open an options trading account today. What's important is that you have put your feet on the path to success. Let's begin with some basic questions.

➢ From Novice to DIY Investor: An Action List

Chapter 6 highlights some of the specific questions your broker will ask when you open your first options trading account. Prior to approaching your broker, there are some steps you can take to prepare yourself:

- Create a personal financial balance sheet showing your assets, liabilities, annual income and expenses, and other information about your financial picture. You can use any type of spreadsheet software; there are also many financial planning tools and software available on the internet and at office supply stores.

- If you are a business owner, create a similar financial balance sheet for your business.

- Identify your current retirement savings balances and accounts.

- Outline your plan for retirement:
  □ At what age would you like to retire? How much will you need to retire comfortably? You can type "retirement savings calculator" into any internet search engine window to find tools that will help you determine your needs.

- Determine your level of confidence in investing:
  □ Have I ever bought stocks or bonds as an independent investor?
  □ How many times per year have I completed investment transactions?
  □ What types of investments make up my investment portfolio?
  □ Have I ever opened any kind of investment account?
  □ On a scale of 1 to 10, how confident am I if someone were to ask me to invest $10,000 in the stock market?

☐ What percentage of my savings and retirement is the result of my independent activity as a private investor?

➢ *Do I need a broker?*

To become an options trader, you will need a specific type of account--an options trading account. Options trading accounts must be opened with a licensed broker. In addition, you must meet some basic requirements. Chapter 6 explains these requirements in detail.

➢ *How much should I invest?*

The good news is that the answer to this question will vary from person to person and from trade to trade. Even better, if you become an investor on the stock market, and you are active in options trading, there may be no upper limit to the amount of money you can invest.

➢ *How much risk should I take on?*

Again, the answer to this question will vary from person to person and from trade to trade. Keep in mind that options trading itself requires the presence of risk in order for an opportunity for investment to exist. At the same time, this does not mean you will necessarily have to expose yourself to extremely high risk. In fact, options trading was developed as a specific method for reducing or eliminating risk. Depending on your skill, your confidence, and the amount of investment capital you have access to, you can choose to expose yourself to higher levels of risk if you are convinced that doing so will result in a greater ROI.

4

INVESTING IN OPTIONS—THE BASICS

Now we have covered most of the basic land-
scape of professional investing. By now you
understand the differences among the many types
of investments that are available--from securities to
derivatives to commodities. You also understand the
difference between putting money into an employer-sponsored managed investment account and
actively pursuing investments yourself by buying
and selling securities on the stock market. Perhaps
at this point, you may already have assembled an
investment portfolio of stocks and bonds and found
a way to reinvest your earnings to ensure you have a
residual income working for you. If so, congratula-
tions--that's great news! If not--congratulations on
taking the first step by reading this book!

Whatever your previous experience in active
investing, this chapter is designed to help you focus
your skills on a very narrow and specific area of
investing--options trading. This chapter will provide

an in-depth definition of options and options contracts and the terms you will encounter daily as you build a successful options trading portfolio.

Options Defined

Securities such as stock in a company, savings bonds, Treasury bills, or hard assets like real estate or other commodities, offer investors the opportunity to own part of a tangible asset. As discussed in Chapter 2, options are derivatives. Their value is not tied directly to the tangible asset represented by the stock certificate; instead, their value is derived from that asset, usually referred to as an underlying asset.

For example, if an investor owns stock in Microsoft Corporation, each share of stock represents his or her financial interest in the goods or services produced and sold by Microsoft Corporation--the greater the value of those goods and services on the market, the more value is assigned to the stock certificate, and the higher the price for each individual share in the company.

Thus, if an investor believes shares of Microsoft are going to increase, he or she can purchase shares of the company at the current market rate. If the shares actually do increase, the value of his or her shares also increases.

Options, on the other hand, are not shares in any tangible asset. They are contracts that give the owner the right--but not the obligation--to buy or sell an underlying asset at a previously agreed price, on or before a previously agreed date.

30 years ago, investors had the opportunity to purchase shares in Microsoft at a much lower share price than its current trading value; those investors who made such a purchase have seen an increase in the value of their investment because shares of Microsoft are now trading at a much higher level. Thus, owning an asset that increases in value is one way to make money through investing.

However, an options trader may use changes in the stock to benefit by deriving further value from stock in his or her investment portfolio. For example, the Microsoft shareholder who bought 100 shares 30 years ago (Investor A) may believe that the value of his stock is going to decline. He has already earned a considerable return on his investment, so to avoid a loss, he may write a put option to sell his shares at a fixed price (the strike price) on a certain date. The strike price is set below the current market value.

At the expiration date, if the value of the stock drops below the strike price, the investor who bought this option (Investor B) has the right to buy the shares at the strike price, which at that point will be higher than the current market value for shares at that time. In this way, Investor A has sold his shares of Microsoft at a price that allowed him to realize his initial investment in the company, while also avoiding losses resulting from the more recent drop in the value of the stock. Thus, the value of the options contract is **derived** from the value of an underlying asset (Microsoft stock), not tied directly to it.

Terminology

Types of Options

There are two types of options contracts.

Physical delivery options
A physical delivery option requires the physical delivery of the underlying asset if the option is exercised at the expiration date.
For example:

- If an investor buys a physical delivery call option for 100 shares of Company A, he must purchase the 100 shares at the strike price from the investor who sold him the option at the time the option is exercised.
- If an investor buys a physical delivery put option for 100 shares of Company A, he must sell the 100 shares at the strike price to the investor who sold him the option at the time the option is exercised.

Cash-settled options
A cash-settled options contract entitles the owner of the contract to receive a payment for the difference between the market value of an underlying asset at

the time the option is exercised and the strike price of that asset, as named in the options contract.

For example:

- If an investor buys a cash-settled call option for 100 shares of Company A, he has the right to receive a cash payment from the seller of the call option for the difference between the strike price of the underlying asset and the market value of the underlying asset at the time the position is closed or the option is exercised.
- If an investor buys a cash-settled put option for 100 shares of Company A, he has the right to receive a cash payment from the seller of the put option for the difference between the strike price of the underlying asset and the market value of the underlying asset at the time the position is closed or the option is exercised.

Many options traders already hold an equity interest in an existing security--such as stock in a company. In these cases, investors may use options contracts in combination with regular securities trading to provide some measure of protection against market volatility. Using the example of Microsoft Investor A above, an investor who intends to liquidate a large part of his stock portfolio that has already paid him sizeable dividends may purchase an options contract to ensure that when he does sell his stock, he will be able to do so at a guaranteed price, regardless of market fluctuations. These investors will likely use a physical delivery options contract.

However, options contracts are classified as derivatives and designed to enable investors with a means of enhancing the value of existing investment portfolios or creating additional sources of investment income. Thus, by investing in cash-settlement options contracts, investors can realize profits from changes in the valuation of existing securities without the risk or expense of buying, owning, or selling the securities themselves. Most options contracts are of the cash-settled variety.

Call Options

In the language of options trading, the term "call," means, "buy." A call option is an options contract that gives an investor the right to buy a certain number of shares of a security at an agreed, pre-determined price during a specified period of time. Generally, an investor will purchase a call option if he believes the share price of the security he is interested in will rise during the time of the options contract. By purchasing the options contract, he guarantees for himself the right to purchase those shares at a price he believes will be lower than the market price by the time the contract expires.

Put Options

In the language of options trading, the term, "put," means, "sell." A put option works the same way a call option works but in the opposite direction. An investor will buy a put option contract when he believes the share price of a security he is interested in selling will be falling during the time the contract is in effect. By purchasing the put option contract, he can agree to a selling price for the shares controlled by the contract that will be higher than the market price by the time the contract expires.

Expiration Date

Every options contract must have an expiration date. The expiration date for an options contract may be a week into the future, a month into the future, or it may expire at the end of the quarter. The expiration date is the date by which the securities controlled by the contract must be either bought or sold. Options contracts may be renewed before the expiration date.

Strike Price

The strike price in an options contract is the purchase price of the shares controlled by a call option or the selling price of the shares controlled by a put option.

Premium

The premium is the amount an investor pays to exercise his rights in an options contract.

Intrinsic Value

The intrinsic value of an options contract is determined by the strike price relative to the projected market value of the underlying securities at the expiration date. Thus, call options have greater intrinsic value the lower their strike price; put options have greater intrinsic value the higher their strike price.

Time Value

Time value refers to the value of an options contract relative to the date the contract was written or most recently renewed. Options contracts must typically be renewed weekly, monthly, or quarterly. The longer the amount of time after the contract is renewed, the less value an options contract has.

Option Styles

Despite the names of the two styles of options contracts, geographical location is irrelevant with regard to which style of options contract investors choose. The two main styles of options contracts are American style and European style. There are also many variations or "exotic" styles.

➢ American style

In an American style options contract, the investors in the contract may exercise their right to buy or sell the shares of the underlying securities at any time during the contract up until the expiration date. The right to exercise calls or puts prior to the expiration date provides options traders with an advantage over less flexible European style contracts. As a result, American style options contracts may carry a higher premium than European style counterparts.

➢ *European style*

In a European style options contract, the investors who are parties to the contract may only exercise their right to buy or sell the shares of the underlying securities on the expiration date of the contract. European style options contracts are the predominant style used on most indexes.

Exotics

Exotic style options contracts allow experienced, professional options traders to include variations of American and European style contracts. These exotic options contracts may use different criteria to determine whether the contract pays. For example, an exotic contract may offer investors the opportunity to profit-based exclusively on whether the share price of a given security rises or falls, with no consideration of how much the share price changes. Again, these exotic options contract variations are generally used by more experienced traders. Although this book is designed for the beginning options trader, the following is a list of some types of exotic options contracts:

- Binary options
- Knock-out options
- Knock-in options
- Barrier options
- Lookback options
- Asian options
- Bermudan options

Buying and Selling Options

Now that you understand the difference between call options and put options, you should also consider that investors can both buy and sell both types of options. Investors can buy or sell either put options or call options. Options buyers are called "holders"; options sellers are called "writers." To understand the dynamics of buying and selling options contracts, let's consider first how buying and selling securities works for investors:

- An investor who buys stock in a company can be said to occupy a "long position" on that stock.
- Conversely, an investor who short-sells stock occupies a "short position" on that stock.

As a result:

- An investor who buys a put option can potentially occupy a short position on the underlying stock if the rights in the options contract are exercised.

44

- An investor who buys a call option can potentially occupy a long position on the underlying stock.

And:

- An investor who sells a put option gives the purchaser the potential to occupy a long position on the underlying stock.
- An investor who sells a call option can potentially occupy a short position on the underlying stock.

The Mechanics of Options Contracts

Let's look at the moving parts of a basic options contract:

- Generally, each options contract controls 100 shares of the underlying asset.

- At any time, there are as many as four participants in an options contract transaction:
  □ an investor who buys puts;
  □ an investor who sells puts;
  □ an investor who buys calls;
  □ an investor who sells calls.

- There are two significant transactions in an options contract:
  □ opening a position;

☐ closing a position.

An options trader may open a position in an options contract by selling (writing) or buying an options contract to either buy or sell assets.

Anytime an investor opens a position by writing an options contract, his broker will match that contract with a potential buyer. Similarly, an investor may open his position by buying a contract that has already been written.

Options traders must also exit the options contract to realize any profit from the transaction and/or to avoid any potential losses. To close a position in an options contract, an options trader will buy back or sell back the options he originally sold or bought.

Options Contracts in Motion

Before we examine options trading in greater detail, let's consider two illustrations that can help you understand the material we have covered so far. We have constructed two scenarios--one featuring a call option and one featuring a put option--so you can see how a well-designed and well-played options contract can help you create a source of investment income.

Scenario 1: Call Option

• The situation:
It is January 1, 2020. You have been studying the performance of Acme Company, and you

are convinced that the value of their stock will increase by the end of the month. Currently, the stock is trading at $45.00 per share. You contact your broker and instruct him to purchase a call option for Acme Company for a strike price of $47.00 for the month of January. Your broker tells you the premium for this option is $2.25. You approve the purchase. Here are the details of your call option contract:

- ☐ The strike price is $47.00.
- ☐ The expiration date is January 17, 2020.
- ☐ The total premium is $225.00 ($2.25 x 100 shares).
- ☐ The call option quote is written as follows: ACME January 47 Call
- ☐ For the call option to be "in-the-money," the price of the shares must increase to $47.00 by the end of January.
- ☐ To break even, the share price must increase to $49.25 so you can make back the money you spent on the premium.
- ☐ To make a profit, the share price by the end of January must be higher than $49.25.

- • The action:
  - ☐ After two weeks, the share price of Acme Company has increased to $60.00.
  - ☐ In addition, because of the rise in share price, the premium for this call option

has increased to $12.00, which means the options contract is now worth $1,200.00.

- Your decisions:
  There are three possible ways to play this options contract:
  □ Because the value of the options contract has increased from $225.00 to $1,200.00, you could close your position by selling the options contract and accepting a cash settlement payment of $975.00, less fees and commissions.
  □ You could exercise your option to buy the underlying shares in Acme Company. The shares are currently trading at $60.00, but your contract guarantees you the right to buy them any time before the expiration date at the strike price of $47.00.
  □ If you believe the share price will continue to go up, you can wait until closer to the expiration date, and then either sell the option contract or purchase the shares at the strike price. However, if the share price falls below $45.00, the contract will expire worthless, and you will lose the $225.00 premium.

Scenario 2: Put Option

- The situation:
  It is January 1, 2020. You have been studying the performance of Acme Company, and you

are convinced that the value of their stock will decrease by the end of the month. Currently, the stock is trading at $45.00 per share. You contact your broker and instruct him to purchase a put option for Acme Company for a strike price of $43.00 for the month of January. Your broker tells you the premium for this option is $2.25. You approve the purchase. Here are the details of your put option contract:

- ☐ The strike price is $43.00.
- ☐ The expiration date is January 17, 2020.
- ☐ The total premium is $225.00 ($2.25 x 100 shares).
- ☐ The call option quote is written as follows: ACME January 43 Put
- ☐ For the put option to be "in-the-money," the price of the shares must fall to $43.00 by the end of January.
- ☐ To break even, the share price must fall to $40.75, so you can make back the money you spent on the premium.
- ☐ To make a profit, the share price by the end of January must be lower than $40.75.

- The action:
  - ☐ After two weeks, the share price of Acme Company has decreased to $30.00.
  - ☐ In addition, because of the steep fall in share price, the premium for this call option has increased to $12.00, which

means the options contract is now worth $1,200.00.

- Your decisions:

  There are three possible ways to play this options contract:

  □ Because the value of the options contract has increased from $225.00 to $1,200.00, you could close your position by selling the options contract and accepting a cash settlement payment of $975.00, less fees and commissions.

  □ You could exercise your option to sell the underlying shares in Acme Company. The shares are currently trading at $30.00, but your contract guarantees you the right to sell them to the writer of the put option contract any time before the expiration date at the strike price of $43.00.

  □ If you believe the share price will continue to continue to drop, you can wait until closer to the expiration date, and then either sell the option contract for what will hopefully be an even higher premium or sell the shares at the strike price. However, if the share price rises above $45.00, the contract will expire worthless, and you will lose the $225.00 premium.

5

WHY SHOULD I INVEST IN OPTIONS?

You could say that risk is the reason investment exists. Without the risk of retiring without money in the bank, no one would be motivated to begin saving for retirement. Many--if not all--businesses and corporations have become successful by inventing or perfecting goods and services that eliminate risk or difficulty in some area of our lives--law firms reduce the risk posed by liability and crime; grocery stores mitigate the risk that we will not have enough food; schools and universities reduce the risk that we will not have the skills and knowledge to compete in the workplace. There is an abundance of risk in the world, and human beings have developed many highly refined responses for successfully addressing those risks.

The stock market is in many ways a means for businesses to address the risks inherent in the global marketplace. Competition, weather, geographical location, and access to resources are the concerns that all businesses face. The stock market provides an open exchange where businesses from around the world can resolve risks and resolve disputes by engaging in mutually beneficial trade. Options trading has always been a part of this practice and was originally developed as an investment tool designed specifically to address risk within the context of global trade. Thus, for any investor, options trading provides some very specific benefits.

Who invests in options?

To some degree, everyone engages in options trading. If you have any kind of an insurance policy, you have already purchased a form of an options contract. For a monthly fee, your auto insurance policy guarantees that if your car is damaged, all the repairs will be paid for. More than likely, the sum total of your insurance premiums costs you less than you would have to pay to repair extensive damage to your vehicle.

Professional investors specialize in options trading for a number of reasons. International investors may engage in options trades to mitigate losses posed by changes in currency exchange rates. Other traders may write options contracts to ensure commodities purchases will take place at "locked in" prices. Some options traders want to hedge against potential losses in their investment portfolios by writing options contracts that allow both buyers and sellers to avoid losses due to changes in market conditions. Still other investors regard options trading as an entire investment strategy unto itself--these prospectors use their knowledge that securities traders want to avoid risk to create a stream of income that consists entirely of options contracts.

Whatever your motivation for investing in options contracts, you should understand their basic function and the risks and benefits inherent to this form of investing.

Options vs. Securities

There are some similarities between options trading and securities trading:

- Both securities and options are traded on SEC-regulated markets.
- Both securities and options are traded through brokers.
- The performance of both securities and options can be followed on stock market indices.

There are also several fundamental differences between options trading and securities trading:

- Each options contract controls 100 shares of equity in the underlying asset. However, equity in a company is sold by the share; the share price of a company as shown on the stock market represents the cost of buying one share of equity in the company.

- Parties to an options contract who exercise their right to either buy or sell the underlying shares may profit from changes in the market value of the shares without having to purchase equity in the company directly. Shareholders do not have any equivalent right to share in the profit of an options trade.

- Options provide a means to reduce risk. Investing in securities involves the risk of losing the capital invested in the company without any equivalent way to mitigate that loss.

- Options traders' main risk is the loss of the premium they paid for the options contract. Traders who own equity in a company risk losing the value of their portfolio if the stocks do not produce a return on investment.

- All options contracts must have an expiration date, after which time they do not retain any value. Stock certificates do not expire unless the company goes out of business.

- If the exact conditions of an options contract are not met by the expiration date, the contract expires worthless. Because stock certificates do not have an expiration date, when they lose value, the investors' portfolios lose value as well.

- Investors who purchase a premium for an options contract do not receive a certificate of ownership in the company. Investors who purchase shares in a company receive a stock certificate; thus, stocks are a tangible asset.

- Purchasing an options contract does not give the investor voting rights or equity in the company unless the investor exercises the right to buy the shares in a call option. Owning shares in a company gives the shareholder certain voting rights in the company.
- There is no limit to the number of options contracts that investors may trade on any company's assets. Shares of stock are sold in a fixed number, which is determined by the issuing company.

Case Studies

Let's review some case studies that illustrate situations in which an options trade may benefit an investor.

1. Compensating for fluctuations in prices and exchange rates

   First, some options contracts may be written to mitigate losses resulting from changes in currency exchange rates. The price of one currency in terms of another currency is known as an exchange rate. As of the writing of this book, the cost to buy 1 British Pound in US Dollars is $1.25; thus, an asset on the British market--Company A--may be trading at 20 British Pounds per share, which is the equivalent of $25. U.S. traders in an international market purchasing assets valued in British pounds may cover their assets with an options contract that allows them to buy the assets at a pre-agreed strike price that reflects the exchange rate currently in effect to offset potential losses posed by fluctuations in that exchange rate. If an options trader in an international market believes the stock price will remain stable, but the exchange rate will fluctuate in favor of the British Pound, he may buy a call option to purchase 100 shares of Company A at $25.00. If the exchange rate fluctuates as expected before the options contract expires, the trader has the right to purchase the underlying asset at the previous exchange rate.

2. Corporate options trading

Next, corporations may engage in options trading when they are considering major commodities purchases in order to avoid losses resulting from possible changes in market conditions.

For example, let's imagine a commercial builder has planned a new development that will include new residences as well as many commercial buildings. The developer has won the bid and can begin construction at the beginning of the following year. However, the state legislature will be passing new environmental laws that will affect the cost of materials and the overall cost of completing the entire development. The total increase in the costs were unknown at the time the contractor won the bid, so the contractor secured the services of a local supplier by signing an agreement stating that the supplier would provide all supplies at current market values. To secure the contract, the developer agreed to pay a fee that was less than what they believed would be the minimum amount of cost increases resulting from the new laws.

Although this example does not represent an options trade on the market, it illustrates how large corporations can use options contracts to make their investments more profitable.

3. Hedging

Third, many day traders who routinely buy and sell securities use options contracts to bolster their earnings, avoid loss, or even make money when stock sales and purchases don't perform the way they had hoped.

"Hedging" is the term used to indicate using an options contract to minimize or avoid potential loses as a result of a decline in share prices. For example, if an investor wants to purchase technology stocks but is concerned that their volatility poses short-term risk, he can buy the stocks in combination with a put option and instruct his broker to exercise the option to sell the stock if it drops below a value that represents a loss to his portfolio.

Alternatively, if a trader owns stock in a company that he believes will be experiencing short-term volatility with no risk of long-term loss, he can construct a strategy using options contracts to earn a short-term gain during the period of volatility.

4. Prospecting

Finally, many investors--commonly known as prospectors--make a living by writing options contracts that help other investors mitigate the risks that are an inherent part of the stock market.

Many options traders frequently use a variety of strategies to generate income from fluctuations in the value of stock prices without purchasing any of the actual stock. Buying shares in a company is more expensive than buying an options contract, especially when you consider that one options contract controls 100 shares of stock. Also known as speculation, an options trader who has predicted a rise in the value of a particular stock can purchase a call option on that stock above the current market value, but below the value he believes it will ultimately reach prior to the expiration date. By selling the call option when the stock price exceeds the strike price, the trader profits from a valuation of stock without the expense of actually buying and selling the shares.

Benefits of Investing in Options

As we have seen, options are extremely versatile financial instruments that can serve the interests of many different types of investors in many different types of investment scenarios. This book is written for the beginning options trader, so the main focus is on stock options. Keep in mind there are other markets in which options traders are active, including foreign currency markets, debt securities, and index options. The world of options trading opens virtually unlimited possibilities for the skilled and disciplined investor. However, trading options contracts not only offers many benefits but also poses some potential risks that are unique to the options market. Before we examine the specifics of opening an options trading account and the specific strategies you may employ, we'll take some time to examine the benefits that options contracts can bring to your investment portfolio, as well as many of the risks inherent in this area of investing.

Less Expensive

Purchasing an options contract is far less expensive than purchasing an equal amount of shares of stock in a company. If an investor wanted to purchase stock in a promising technology company that was currently trading at $35 per share, he would have to pay $3,500 for 100 shares of stock. However, assuming the premium for a call option on the same stock is $3.50 per share, the same investor can use that $3,500 to purchase 10 call option contracts which would control 1,000 shares of the same stock.

While a share of stock may give the investor a controlling interest and value tied directly to the company's underlying assets, options contracts allow investors to control potentially hundreds of shares at a fraction of the cost.

"Leveraged" Investment Returns

Because options contracts allow investors to control hundreds of shares during any given transaction, options trading can allow investors to leverage the volume of the market and provide greater returns for a smaller up-front investment.

Using the example above, assume both investors were interested in a six-month return, and assume the stock values increased to $50 by the end of the six-month period. The investor who purchased 100 shares would see an increase in the value of his investment from $3,500 to $5,000, for a total gain of $1,500--a 43% return on investment. Meanwhile, the investor who purchased 10 call option contracts sees an increase in the value of his investment from $3,500 to $50,000, less the $5,000 he paid for the contracts, for a total gain of $41,500--a 1,186% return.

Provides a Source of Revenue

Investing in options contracts also provides several ways for investors who are already active in the stock market to create an additional source of revenue:

- Using a combination of call options and put options, investors can protect their existing portfolios from losses resulting from declines in market prices.
- A combination of well-timed and well-planned options contracts can help traders increase income on current investments by capitalizing on market changes.
- Investors who are interested in assembling a profitable stock portfolio can increase the value of that portfolio by using options contracts to purchase stock at reduced prices.
- Finally, as we have seen in examples illustrating prospecting, income from options trades on assets the investor does not own can produce an additional source of income to supplement the value of his or her existing portfolio.

Mitigates Investment Risk

Because options are not tied directly to the underlying assets of any given company, options traders do not have to tolerate as much risk of losing real capital. More importantly, because options contracts do not obligate any of the market participants to actually buy or sell anything, the risks associated with non-performing contracts are virtually absent.

Provides a "Hedge" Against Loss

Options were designed as a financial instrument to help investors insure themselves against the uncertainties of the market. Although they are very flexible and adaptable financial instruments, their primary purpose remains their most valuable purpose. The volatility and uncertainty of the stock market--especially in the contemporary economic climate--poses potentially unlimited risks across the board. By using options contracts judiciously, skilled investors can not only virtually eliminate risk from their portfolio but can also use options to turn potential market losses into financial gains.

Risks of Investing in Options

The overwhelming popularity of investing in stock options results from their seemingly endless versatility. However, as with all areas of investing, options traders must also be able to tolerate risk. In fact, depending on the level of your options trading account and the complexity of your investment strategies, your broker may require you to deposit funds in a margin account to insure the brokerage firm against any losses in capital in the event an options trade does not go the way you planned. This section first outlines some of the general risks common to all options traders, then lists many of the risks specific to certain options trading strategies and positions.

Time-sensitive

Stocks do not have expiration dates, so investors can decide to "wait out" periods during which the stock loses value until it is back "in-the-money."

However, to execute an options contract successfully, the parties to the contract must ensure that all transactions are completed within very specific time limits and deadlines. All options contracts have expiration dates, so if the contract approaches the expiration date and the terms of the contract are not met--that is, if the stock does not reach the desired value or strike price--the contract will expire worthless and the trader will forfeit the cost of purchasing the contract--the premium--without realizing any profit.

In addition, as the options contract approaches its expiration date, it loses value. This is known as time decay, and if part of your strategy is to sell an options contract before the expiration date, you will have to consider how time decay affects this strategy.

Price-sensitive

Investors who trade stocks have 2 main concerns-- the share price of the stock at the time of purchase and the share price of that stock over time. As long as the share price increases--regardless of how much-- the investment will continue to be profitable.

Options traders must not only select an expiration date for their options contract, they must also select a strike price. An options trader who is betting that the share price of a stock will fall by buying a put option must not only be right about the direction of the stock price, he must also be right about the amount of that decrease.

Similarly, an options trader betting on the increase of the share price of a given asset must accurately predict how much the share price will increase. In either of these cases, the trader can be right about the direction of the stock, but if he selects a strike price that is either too high or too low, the contract will expire worthless, and he will lose the cost of the premium.

Short-term Investment

Unlike a traditional IRA or 401(k) in which investors pool their money into diversified portfolios of securities that pay out dividends over years or even decades, options contracts expire within months, weeks, or even days. Thus, options trading requires the active involvement of the trader to ensure profitability and to avoid unexpected loss, which in some cases can be unlimited.

Intangible Asset

Options contracts are investments that are derived from the value of hard assets and securities. Although an options contract has "intrinsic value," this value only represents the potential profit a trader can earn from the contract before it expires. Unlike stocks, bonds, and commodities, options contracts have no real value, and options traders do not receive certificates or earn voting rights unless they use the contract to purchase the underlying shares in the contract before the expiration date.

Complex Strategies

Building a profitable portfolio of securities requires knowledge of investing, an understanding of how the market works, and the ability to know when to buy and when to sell. However, the strategies involved in securities trades are fairly straightforward when compared to the strategies employed by many options traders. Although options contracts provide great flexibility and adaptability, often the benefits of options contracts can only be realized by utilizing fairly complex strategies.

Specific Risks for the Options Trader

Depending on your level of experience and expertise as an options trader, you may place yourself in a position that leaves you open to a greater degree of risk. Every options trade is unique, and every options trader has his or her own preferred strategies for creating profitability from the market. Although it is not possible to predict every scenario or calculate the odds for every conceivable risk, the following list indicates which positions and strategies involve greater risk:

Risks for option holders:

1. Option holders risk losing the entire investment in the premium if the terms of the contract are not met at expiration and they let the contract expire.

2. OTM contracts lose value as they move further out of the money and further from the expiration date. Holders risk losing not only the premium but also the ability to mitigate loss by selling the contract on a secondary market.

3. Holders of European-style options cannot realize profits prior to the exercise period before the expiration date. As a result, they may have to forgo potential profits that may occur prior to the exercise period. In addition, if the options contract appears to be moving toward a loss, they may be forced to accept

the loss of the premium if there is no secondary market on which to sell the contract.

4. Investors who purchase options with an "automatic exercise" feature may have to take some type of action to ensure the contract is exercised according to instructions. They may also risk losing profit or even capital if changes in the market render the terms of the automatic exercise less effective.

5. All options holders are subject to unexpected outside restrictions imposed by the Securities and Exchange Commission (SEC), the Options Clearing Corporation (OCC), or the options market in which they are trading.

Risks for options writers:

1. Any trader who writes an option is liable for losses that may occur if an assignment is exercised. For example, if a trader writes a put option, the option is in-the-money prior to the expiration date, and the buyer of that put option exercises his rights under the contract, then the writer will have to either purchase the underlying asset or pay the cash settlement amount. This risk is a particular concern for writers of American-style options which can be exercised at any time prior to the expiration date.

2. Any trader who writes a covered call may not realize any profit in excess of the strike price

if the underlying asset closes above the strike price at expiration; in addition, the writer is still vulnerable to losses if the share price drops below market value.

3. Any trader who writes an uncovered call (a call option on an asset in which he does not own any interest) runs the risk of potentially unlimited losses. For example, if the trader writes an uncovered call at a premium of $2 for stock in Company D with a strike price of $25, he will receive a premium of $200. However, if the stock price rises dramatically--for example to $65--he may be required to deliver the underlying asset at the strike price. This can cause substantial losses if he does not already own the shares in the underlying asset.

4. Any trader who writes an uncovered put (a put option on an asset in which he does not own any interest) runs the risk of potentially unlimited losses. For example, if the trader writes an uncovered put at a premium of $2 for stock in Company E with a strike price of $25, he will receive a premium of $200. However, if the stock price drops dramatically--for example to $1--he may be required to purchase the underlying asset at the strike price of $25.

5. In certain situations, a trader who writes uncovered calls or puts may be required

to deposit funds into his or her brokerage account to cover potential losses.

6. Option writes may be assigned an exercise without notification. As a result, they may be required to purchase or deliver the underlying interest or the cash settlement amount without the opportunity to close the transaction to offset the loss.

What do I need to know?

By now, you have completed an introduction to the basic terminology used in investment generally and in options trading specifically. You have considered your goals as an investor and thought about how your background and experience qualify you to trade options. If the prospect of enhancing your portfolio's profitability with an options trading account sounds appealing, that's great!

But success in investing requires knowledge, diligence, and preparation, so before you contact a broker to make your first trade, take a few moments to answer these questions to assess how options trading fits into your overall investment plan:

1. What are my investment goals?
   Review the information in Chapter 3. Are you interested in launching a career as a professional options trader, or are you interested in learning about options trading

as a means of supplementing your existing portfolio?

Are you interested in saving for retirement or creating a source of income-based entirely on professional investing?

If you haven't already, you should create a balance sheet of both your personal and professional financial pictures. Your balance sheet should include a statement of assets and liabilities; income and expenses; as well as information about projected areas of growth.

As you move forward, this information will help you clarify your own financial needs and goals. It will also help you communicate more effectively with your broker and your fellow traders.

2. What kind of investor am I?

There are many types of investors from college students and homemakers who save their paychecks in savings accounts to professional hedge fund managers who make executive decisions on Wall Street. Don't let the terminology of options trading intimidate you. Whether you are a beginning investor, a professional with considerable financial literacy, or a full-time DIY investment pro, there is a place for you in the standardized options trading market.

3. Why do I want to become an options trader? Considering your motivation to enter the world of professional options trading will help you focus your efforts, especially early on. As you read Chapter 6, you will see that the options market is well-regulated and standardized. If you are prepared to blaze a maverick trail through the options market, that's great--your enthusiasm and dedication will surely pay off. But remember, options traders must conduct trades through a licensed broker, so you won't have to go it alone. What's more, the more clear you are about your reasons for entering the options market, the easier it will be for you to select a trading level and options strategies that will be most helpful in achieving those goals.

4. How do I get started?

Opening an options trading account is the first step in your options trading career. The first 5 chapters of this book have laid a foundation that has covered the basics of investing, as well as many of the concepts and concerns specific to the field of options trading. Chapter 6 will discuss the specifics of opening an options trading account.

6

GETTING STARTED

Now that you have covered the basics of investing and of options trading, it's time to get started. Options trading is a highly specialized and complex area of securities trading. While it may be possible to engage in OTC options contract trades, becoming proficient and making money by trading options requires forethought and planning. Before we examine the most common options trading strategies, you should become familiar with basic terminology common to options trading. In addition, you will need to complete a few items on your to-do list before you complete your first options contract transaction.

This chapter begins by walking you through the basics of opening an options trading account. Next, we will examine the basic "moving parts" of the options contract. Finally, we'll discuss in some detail the general skills you will be drawing upon as you move into this area of securities investment.

Opening an Options Trading Account

If you are reading this book, chances are you have opened--at least once in your lifetime--a regular checking account or savings account at a bank. Most banks make it fairly easy to open an account, make deposits and withdrawals, and write checks or use debit or credit cards to pay for things. There are not a lot of prerequisites for opening a regular checking or savings accounts either--if you can supply a name and address, a form of government-issued identification, and a social security number, you can usually be up and running in no more than an hour.

Business banking accounts pose a little more of a challenge. Although the process is similar to opening a regular bank account, opening a business account does have one prerequisite account holders must meet--they must have a business.

If you have an employer-sponsored retirement savings account--usually either a 401(k) or an IRA--you may have at least some indirect experience opening an investment account. Often, your human resources department employs people who have been hired to complete this process for you. You may have been asked to select one of several types of investment accounts where your monthly contributions will be deposited. You may even recall an afternoon during which an investment advisor provided a presentation covering the differences among the various types of retirement accounts, but if you are like most people, your involvement in this process was likely limited to checking a box on the registration form.

Of course, it is not uncommon for people to take some individual action regarding investments. For example, if you are self-employed or if your employer does not provide any retirement benefits, you may have contacted an investment broker individually to ask them about the types of options that are available for individuals who want to save for retirement. If this is the case, you may have a greater degree of familiarity with investment terms and types of investment accounts.

Others may have worked with their personal bankers to put money away for retirement. If so, you may have opened a mutual fund account, a money market account, or a certificate of deposit.

Regardless of your degree of previous experience in financial investing, options trading requires that you open an options trading account with a licensed financial broker. In addition, because options trading is a fairly complex area of investment, not everyone is automatically qualified to open such an account.

The federal Securities and Exchange Commission (SEC) has formulated regulations for ensuring accountability among options traders and brokers. Before you can open an options trading account, your broker will ask you to complete an options agreement. This agreement is designed to help your broker understand your background and experience as a financial investment professional. These requirements have been established not to prevent people from building wealth through options trading, but to provide safeguards to ensure that investors who may lack the required knowledge and experience do not suffer potentially devastating investment losses.

The following sections provide information about some of the things your broker will need to know before you can open an options trading account.

Questions from Your Broker

- What are your investment objectives? Possible answers may include:
    □ capital preservation
    □ income
    □ wealth building or growth
    □ speculation

- How much experience do you have as a trader?

- What types of trades have you completed in the past? Stocks only or stocks and options?

- How many trades do you make each year?

- What is the average value of the trades you have made?

- What other experience or knowledge of investment do you have?

- Do have any experience with any of the following types of investments:
  - ☐ stocks
  - ☐ bonds
  - ☐ mutual funds/ETFs
  - ☐ futures
  - ☐ cash alternatives
  - ☐ real estate
  - ☐ annuities
  - ☐ alternative investments

- What are the details of your personal finances?
  - ☐ What is the value of your liquid assets?
  - ☐ What is your net worth?
  - ☐ Are you employed? If so, who is your employer, and what is your occupation?
  - ☐ What is your annual income?

- What kind of options are you interested in trading?

Determining your Trading Level

Chapter 3 outlined some of the basic tools and methods you can use to complete a work-up of your current financial condition. Before you approach a broker about opening an options trading account, you should reread Chapter 3 and complete a complete diagnostic examination of your current financial picture, including a general plan for your financial future, your savings and wealth-building goals and needs, as well as any other concerns or information that may be relevant to the kinds of questions or the type of information your broker will ask for.

Assuming you and your broker agree that you are qualified to open an options trading account and begin buying and selling stock options, there is one additional consideration that your broker will have to make: the trading level that will be assigned to your account.

The practice of identifying and assigning trading levels was developed to protect the interests of both investors and brokers. Not only in options trading but in the world of investments generally, less experienced investors and brokers are more susceptible to taking unwise and unnecessary risks in the hope of gaining greater financial reward, often unsuccessfully. Thanks to regulations enforced by the SEC, brokers can be held liable if they take advantage of inexperienced investors, so the practice of assigning trading levels works to protect the interests of everyone. Although this practice is used throughout professional options trading, there are neither any absolute policies nor any specific requirements for determining how to assign any given investor to a trading level, nor are there any specific regulatory definitions for each of the levels. However, the following descriptions can help you prepare for talking to your broker about an options trading account that is right for you:

➢ *Level 1*

This is an entry-level options trading account. Traders at this level will have a limited ability to engage in options trading. Generally, Level 1 traders will be allowed to buy a put option or sell a call option on any underlying securities in which the trader already owns an interest.

➢ *Level 2*

A Level 2 options trading account allows traders all the same rights as Level 1 account holders. In addition, Level 2 account holders may also be allowed to buy call options or put options in underlying securities in which they have no interest.

➢ *Level 3*

At Level 3, traders retain the rights of both Levels 1 and 2, but can now also begin to conduct transactions that involve margin trading, or trades that require a deposit in the investor's brokerage account in the event losses on the trade exceed the amount of the cost of the premiums. At Level 3, traders may use strategies such as creating spreads and selling covered puts.

➢ *Level 4*

At Level 4, traders again retain access to all the functions of Levels 1, 2, and 3 accounts. However,

Level 4 traders are approved for the riskiest of options trading strategies:

- writing uncovered calls and puts;
- writing uncovered straddles;
- writing uncovered strangles.

➢ *Level 5*

Not every brokerage firm offers Level 5 accounts. Level 5 traders are generally approved for unlimited options trading as long as they are able to deposit sufficient funds in their margin account to cover the broker for potential losses.

Learning the Basics

Predicting the Direction of the Market

As in all areas of investment, options trading involves risk. Success in options trading requires not only that the investor understand those risks, but also that he or she can identify which risks apply to which situation and how much can be tolerated without realizing any major losses. Some investment risks are specific to the options trading profession; other risks apply across the board to all investors. Options traders compete in a niche market, but success in this field requires an understanding of how the market works, how market fundamentals affect the performance of individual stocks, and what that means to the options trader.

Understanding how to analyze the market begins with understanding the various types of risks that apply across-the-board in the investment world. We'll identify risks specific to the various types of options strategies later. Many of the risks involve the trading of securities generally, such as the relative liquidity resources of a company and industry conditions specific to that company's business products. Other risks result from the state of the economy, which can be affected by many different forces within and outside the market. Supply and demand within the options markets themselves, as well as in other related markets, can also affect the types of strategies an options trader will select.

Skilled traders must be able to assess the volatility, liquidity, and efficiency of markets generally; of specific stocks and other assets; and of options markets, all of which can affect the cost of options premiums. Consideration of the quality and liquidity of various options markets at any given time, as well as the degree of familiarity with the procedures of options trading, can help the beginning options trader assess where his efforts will be spent most profitably.

That's a lot to take in, but if you are embarking on a career as an options trader, you should already have some familiarity with the basics of securities trading. Let's consider some of the elements that should be considered before you contact your broker to conduct your first opening transaction.

Market Analysis

When considering the term market analysis, we should consider the term, "market" in two contexts. "Market" may apply to the specific customers or conditions in which any business or industry hopes to establish itself. In terms of investing, "market" may refer to the entire stock market or a specific area, index, or niche of the stock market. Both of these terms have relevance to the options trader.

Using the first example, industry leaders may conduct a market analysis before attempting to sell shares to investors. A well-designed market analysis will consider many factors that may directly affect the potential success of the business, such as the demographics of the target market, the needs of the target market, the size and constitution of competing businesses, potential challenges facing the market, and regulations affecting businesses and industries in the given market. For example, if a medical equipment company wants to open a manufacturing plant in the American Southwest, a market analysis may include an examination of the demographics of the potential customers for its products, including age, income, health-related factors, etc. This analysis may also consider the effect of local business regulations and taxation policies on the ability of the company to be profitable. Thus, a market analysis is an important tool that business owners use prior to an initial public offering.

Similarly, an options trader may need to conduct a market analysis to determine the potential future performance of a given stock or other security to ensure he or she understands what options strategy would be most appropriate at any given time. In this context, "market" refers to the stock market itself, or the options market in which the trader is active. For example, if an options trader were to invest in a call option for Company C, examining Company's C market analysis, as in the first example, might be one tool the trader could use to assess the value of that company's stock. Of course, the stock market involves the performance of more than just one company, so a sound market analysis for the purpose of options trading is a different type of market analysis than what a company might utilize to determine its own profitability. For the options trader, a market analysis requires the use of a combination of several tools and sources of information to understand how the stock market is moving. We will examine some of those methods below.

Trend Lines

A trendline is a fairly simple tool used by technical analysts to determine the current direction of market prices for any given stock. As its name implies, a trendline is created to help an analyst determine the direction in which a stock is trending. To create a trendline, the analyst needs at least two points on a chart showing price changes in share value. The points can represent one-minute intervals, five-minute intervals, daily intervals, weekly intervals, or non-time-based intervals. Thus, if the share price of Company C is trading at $25 on Monday, at $30 on Wednesday, and at $40 on Friday, the trendline will indicate an upward movement of the market value of that share price. Trendlines can be drawn to show the changes in share value at opening, closing, high, and low, using whatever time interval the trader may need to consider. Multiple trend lines comparing highs and lows create what analysts call "channels" that can help traders identify when to enter or exit a particular options strategy. Though fairly simple to create, trendlines need to be updated fairly frequently as new information continually arrives.

Put-Call Ratio (PCR)

The Put-Call Ratio, or PCR, is another tool traders use to gauge and predict the future direction of the market price of any given stock. As with trendlines, PCR's are fairly easy to create. A PCR is determined by dividing the total number of put options traded on assets by the total number of call options traded on assets. Different PCR values are available from any of the options exchanges and include total PCR, equity-only PCR, and index-only PCR. Individual options traders usually trade in equities, so to avoid PCR values that may skew their ability to predict market behavior, most individual traders will use equity-only PCR values when determining options trading strategies.

Volatility Index

There are many indexes that measure market volatility. The CBOE volatility index, also called the VIX, uses options dates to predict the future direction of the markets. VIX is particularly useful for options traders because it measures implied volatility, which is one of the factors used to determine the cost of options contracts.

Standard Deviation

In statistics, the standard deviation is a value used to determine the degree to which, on average, all the values of a given set of values are either higher or lower than the average of all the values. The greater the degree to which the values deviate from the average value of the entire set, the greater the standard deviation.

In finance, standard deviation is used to assess the volatility of a given stock or security. For example, for any given stock, data points are set up to measure its rate of return over a year. The degree to which those data points deviate from the total average rate of return, the more volatile the stock.

Fundamental Analysis

Fundamental analysis is a method of assessing the value of any given stock—and predicting its future performance—by measuring its intrinsic value. The intrinsic value of a stock can be measured by considering concrete factors, such as the earnings, expenses, assets, and liabilities of the company that issued the stock; conditions currently affecting the economy; conditions currently affecting the industry in which the company operates; and any relevant, concrete information that can shed light on how these conditions may affect the value of share prices in the future.

Fundamental analysis makes 3 assumptions:

1. Current stock prices do not necessarily reflect any indication of past or future performance.
2. Market performance is random rather than cyclical.
3. Technical analysis (discussed below) can lead to self-fulfilling prophecies that constitute another factor affecting price share and future performance.

Technical Analysis

Technical analysis is another established method of assessing the value of securities. Technical analysis takes an entirely different approach than fundamental analysis. A technical analyst assumes that the share price of any given security is the sum total of any fundamental analysis that may be conducted; thus, technical analysis takes fundamental analysis as a given. The main concern of technical analysis is the historical performance of that share price over time. Technical analysis attempts to predict the future performance of any given stock by analyzing that stock's past historical behavior with regard to trading volume, price movement, and other factors.

Technical analysis makes three assumptions:

1. All of the considerations of fundamental analysis are already represented in the price of the stock.
2. Changes in stock prices follow trends.
3. Market movements follow cycles.

Designing a Trading Plan

All this theory aside, there really is a practical reason that options traders should understand how to use some of the basic tools of market analysis. Chapter 8 of this book discusses some of the most important "do's and don'ts" of options trading, and maintaining a sound strategy that includes an exit plan may be the most important of all of them.

Options trading is fundamentally different from standard securities trading. A securities trader who wants to purchase stock in a company that will provide a long-term investment will necessarily be less concerned with strategies and exit plans, because his goal is to purchase stock that has tangible value, with an intent to keep it in his portfolio. Options-trading, on the other hand, is a short-term investment strategy whose main goal is to buy and sell securities as quickly as possible to create a source of revenue derived from changes in market conditions.

If you plan to go on a road trip on your next vacation, you would probably spend some time planning your destination, your route, and backup plans in the event of an emergency. Thus, your options trading strategy should be the planned route for your road trip from opening transaction to closing transaction.

➢ *Identify target stocks*

Before you even think about what type of strategy to employ, you will have to identify which stocks or other securities have the potential to generate income via an options trade. As an options trading account holder, you will likely already have an investment portfolio. Especially if you are a Level 1 trader, this may the best place to begin your search since Level 1 traders are required to own the stock on which they write or buy options contracts. If your options trading account is Level 2 or above, you may already have some experience in buying or selling covered calls or puts. If this is the case, then review your previous options trades--either on your own or with the assistance of your broker--to determine the types of securities you have traded in the past.

Of course, you may have no direct experience trading options contracts at all. However, anyone with experience buying and selling securities and building an investment portfolio already has the fundamental skills and knowledge to search for, locate, and analyze stocks that have the potential for generating a profitable return. Your task as an options trader will be to use your skills as a stock analyst to identify those stocks that show the potential for profit over a much shorter term.

➢ *Analyze behavior*

Now that you have located the stocks for which you want to write or buy options contracts, you will have to analyze the behavior of those stocks to determine how their value will change in the short-term. Any of the tools discussed above may be useful in this regard--trendlines, PCRs, and technical analysis can help you determine past and potential future changes in share price.

You should also analyze the securities in your existing portfolio to determine whether an options trading strategy may allow you to increase the revenue they are already generating.

➢ *Determine strike price and expiration date*

Once you have made a determination about the direction of the share price of the stock you have selected, you will have to settle on a specific strike price and expiration date. This step has been standardized by the options trading markets, so you will not have to struggle with identifying precisely how far above or below the market price to set your strike price, or on which day to set the expiration date--these variables are set by the market.

For example, if you want to select a strike below the current trading value, your selections may be limited to increments of $2.00. So, if the current trading value of the stock is $45.00, you may be able to select a strike price of $43.00 0r $41.00. In addition, expiration dates are standardized, as well; generally, options contracts expire on the third Friday of the contract month.

➢ Determine strategy

By now, you have identified the stock on which you want to trade options; you have determined the direction you believe the value of the share price will take; you have identified the amount by which you believe the share price will change; and you have determined a date by which this change in value will take place. These are the fundamental bits of information necessary for developing a profitable strategy.

Success in options trading lies in understanding the different types of strategies in which options contracts can be deployed, then choosing or assembling the strategy most appropriate to your particular investment concern. Chapter 7 examines several standard options trading strategies.

7

SPECIFIC STRATEGIES FOR INVESTING IN OPTIONS

By now, you should have a much clearer idea of where options trading fits in relation to the broad spectrum of activity you will encounter as a securities investor. As you can see, securities trading itself encompasses a broad spectrum of financial activity, and the better educated you are about everything from industry knowledge to politics, to economics, to science and technology, to real estate, to popular culture, the more well-equipped you will be to assess the potential value of securities over time.

Approaching the stock market with a general education about investment basics is a great place to start, but each segment and index within the stock market and every form of investment requires additional, specialized knowledge. Options trading is no different.

Now that you have completed a financial self-assessment, determined your financial goals, formulated an investment plan, and opened an options trading account, you should take some time to learn about the most common strategies used by professionals in the options trading industry. This chapter provides detailed descriptions and examples of nine common strategies used in options trading.

Strategies overview

The nine strategies discussed in this chapter are fairly standard variations of the numerous ways investors use options contracts to generate income, mitigate risk, and hedge against losses. Remember that all of these strategies are based upon the four basic dynamics of options trading, as outlined in Chapter 4:

- Buying put options
- Buying call options
- Selling put options
- Selling call options

The actual type of contract and strategy you use in daily trading may involve one, several, or all of these strategies, depending on the needs and goals of the individual investors, the type of underlying securities you are trading, and conditions affecting the market. Regardless, all investors will benefit from a thorough study of the most commonly used options trading strategies before contacting a broker.

Covered Call

A covered call option may be used by investors for two primary reasons—to generate income by selling a call option and short selling the stock as the share price increases and to protect against a short-term drop in the value of the stock.

To use this strategy, the investor must first purchase shares in a security. After buying the shares, the investor sells one call option for every 100 shares he or she has purchased. This strategy is called a covered call because if the investor who buys the call option decides to purchase the underlying shares, the investor who sold the call is "covered"--he or she already owns the shares represented in the contract.

For example, an investor buys 100 shares in Company XYZ for $25 per share. At the same time, he sells a call option for those shares with a strike price of $27. The investor receives a premium for selling the call option. In addition, if the stock price moves above the strike price, he will be able to sell the stock he bought at $25 per share at the higher strike price of $27.00 per share. If the stock price drops back below the strike price, the investor will be protected against a loss in the share value.

Married Put

This options contract is similar to a covered call but really serves only one purpose—to act as an insurance policy against near-term loss in the value of the underlying stock. A married put option is an options contract that gives the investor the right to sell shares at an agreed price at a predetermined date if the stock covered by the contract drops below a pre-agreed value. This strategy is called a "married" put because the options contract and the shares are purchased from the broker at the same time. A married put strategy decreases the overall value of the investor's interest in the underlying stock by the cost of the premium to purchase the option contract, but the married put also insures the investor against losses resulting from any unforeseen drop in the value of the underlying stock.

Let's say an investor identified stock in Company ABC as a good investment because of its potential for long-term growth. One way to capitalize on this investment is simply to buy and hold the stock. But if the value of the stock were to drop significantly, that investment could turn into a major loss. A married put strategy can act as an insurance policy against losses resulting from a drop in share value.

Using the example above, let's say Company ABC is trading at $35.00 per share. The investor believes the stock will increase in value and buys 100 shares at a total cost of $3,500.00. However, the investor is also concerned about losses if the price drops, so he also buys a $35.00 put option. The put option is priced at $1.00 per share, for a total of $100.00. For this strategy to be considered a married put, the investor buys the shares and the option at the same time and instructs his broker to sell the shares if the option is exercised.

Now, the investor knows that as long as the stock price increases, he will continue to profit from the investment. He will have less of a profit by the amount he spends to purchase the put option (in this case, $100 per 100 shares), but if the value of the share price rises above $36.00, the rest of his earnings by using this strategy will be profit. In addition, if the share price drops below $35.00, the investor will be protected against the loss in value because his put option gives him the right to sell the shares at the same price at which he bought them.

Bull Call Spread

A "call spread" is a term used to describe the difference—the "spread"—between the strike prices of two call option contracts. Investors use a bull call spread strategy when they are "bullish" on the underlying asset—i.e., they believe the shares controlled by the options contract will rise in value.

Using a bull call spread strategy, an investor identifies a security he or she believes will rise in price over a specific period of time. The investor then buys one call option for the asset with a strike price above the underlying asset's current market value and sells a second call option with an even higher strike price. Both call options should have the same expiration date.

The investor pays a premium to buy the call option with the lower strike price. But he receives a premium for selling the call option with the higher strike price. As a result, he has used call options to create a "spread" for the projected increase of the stock's value—the difference between the lower strike price and the higher strike price. At the same time, he has reduced his net cost of employing this call option strategy by buying one call option and selling another.

Next, at the expiration date of the options contracts, if the stock price has dipped beneath the lower strike price, the investor simply lets the options contracts expire. He loses only the net value of buying the options spread. If the stock's value has risen above the higher strike price, he can exercise his option under the first contract and purchase the shares at a price lower than the current market value. Of course, the second options contract is still active, so he will have to sell the shares, but he will have to sell them for the strike price set in the second options contract, rather than the current market value. The money earned from this investment strategy is the difference between the lower strike price and the higher strike price, less the net cost of the premiums for the options contracts.

Thus, using this strategy, an investor can limit potential losses to only the net premium of the two competing options contracts. However, if the stock price rises higher than the second strike price, the investor's earnings on the deal are capped at that strike price.

To illustrate, let's say stock in Company A is currently trading at $20.00 per share. The investor believes the price of the stock will rise in the near term. She decides to use a bull call spread to allow her to capitalize on the increase in the share value while limiting her potential losses.

So, she buys a call option on Company A with a strike price of $22.00. The premium for this call option is $1.00 per share, for a total of $100.00. At the same time, she sells a call option with a strike price of $24.00. The premium for this call option is $0.75 per share, for a total of $75.00. Thus, the total net cost of the premium, per 100 shares of the underlying asset, is $25.00, with losses and gains limited by the upper and lower strike prices of $22.00 and $24.00.

Now, if the price of this stock at the expiration date of this options strategy is trading below the lower strike price of $22.00, the investors can let the entire options spread expire worthless. There is no value on buying the shares at a cost higher than their current trading price, so the investor loses the $25.00 she spent to purchase the spread.

Alternatively, if the price of the stock at expiration is trading at a level higher than $24.00, the investor can exercise her first call option and buy the stock for $22.00. However, because the second call option at $24.00 is still active, the marketplace will assign this option. But the investor can sell the shares she bought at the lower strike price of $22.00 for the higher strike price of $24.00. As a result, she profits on the purchase and sale of the underlying asset in the amount of the difference between the two strike prices--$2.00 per share. Although this strategy can limit losses, its main disadvantage is that the investor's gains are limited to the amount that can be earned by selling shares at the higher of the two strike prices.

Bear Put Spread

Investors use a bear put strategy when they are "bearish" about the underlying asset, i.e., they believe the value of the underlying shares will decline. To create a bear put spread, an investor targets a security he believes will decline moderately in value over a specified period of time. The investor then buys a put option at a strike price above the current market value of the underlying asset and sells a second put option with a strike price below the current market value, but with the same expiration date as the options contract with the higher strike price. The cost of this strategy is the net difference between the premium paid to purchase the option with the higher strike price, and the premium received from selling the put option with the lower strike price.

If the underlying asset closes below the lower strike price at the expiration date, the investor realizes a profit equal to the difference between the two strike prices, less the net cost of the premiums.

This strategy allows an investor to profit from a fluctuation in the value of a given stock without the expense of actually purchasing and selling the stock itself—the cost of this strategy is limited only to the net premium for setting up the options spread. In addition, the investor risks losing only the cost of the net premium since he has not purchased any of the underlying assets.

Of course, if the stock closes at a price that is far lower than the lower of the two strike prices, the investor will not realize any additional profit. In addition, the put option the investor has sold may be assigned early—i.e., the holder of that option may exercise his right to sell the shares before the expiration date.

Let's say stock for Company XYZ is currently trading at $25 per share. An options trader is bearish on this stock and believes its value will decline in the short-term, so he decides to use a bear put spread. He buys a put option contract with a strike price of $28 at a cost of $2.50 per share, for a total of $250.00. At the same time, he sells a put option contract with a strike price of $25.00 at cost of $1.25 per share, for a total of $125.00. The net cost of setting up the spread is $125.00.

Now, at the expiration date of the contract, if the stock is trading below $25.00, the investor will be able to profit on a sale of the underlying shares by the amount of the difference between the two strike prices, less the cost of setting up the spread. In this case, the difference between the two strike prices is $3.00. Multiplied by 100 shares, the difference is $300.00. After subtracting the $125.00 cost of setting up the spread, the net profit for the trader is $175 per options contract.

Protective Collar

This strategy is utilized when an investor has already realized a substantial profit by investing in an underlying asset. The goal of the protective collar is to allow the investor to protect the gains he has realized when the market begins to show signs that the value of the underlying asset may soon decline.

To create a protective collar, an investor purchases a put option with a strike price below the current market value of the underlying assets in which he currently has equity. At the same time, he sells a call option with a strike price slightly above the current market value of the same securities. Both options contracts have the same expiration date. Often, because both of these options are "out of the money," the net premium will likely not cost the investor anything and may even result in a net profit for the investor.

If the stock dips beneath the strike price of the put option, the investor can sell his shares in the company at a strike price that guarantees he will retain most of the value of his investment.

The risk is that the call option the investor has sold potentially caps his earnings from gains in the stock--if the stock closes above the strike price of the call option at the expiration date, the shares in the underlying assets will be purchased at the lower price. The investor will be faced with capped earning potential, and if the stock unexpectedly surges, the investor will not be able to realize any additional profit.

Essentially, this strategy combines a covered call and a married put. Let's say an investor had previously purchased stock at $30.00 per share. Since purchasing the stock, the share price has increased to $75.00 per share, representing a large, as yet unrealized profit for the investor. Although the investor believes the stock may increase in value over the long-term, he is concerned about losses in the short term, so he decides to use a protective collar.

To employ this strategy, the investor buys enough put options to cover his shares, each with a strike price of $72.00. At the same time, he sells an equal number of call options with a strike price of $85.00. Let's say the cost of the $72 put options was $1.50 per share and the cost of the $85.00 call options was $0.75 per share. The nest cost of the premiums is $75.00 per contract.

If the stock closes beneath $72.00 at expiration, the investor limits his losses. By selling his shares at $72.00, he realizes the profit on the initial investment which he bought at $30.00 per share without incurring any further depreciation in the value of the stock. The drawback is that if the stock surges and the share price at the expiration date exceeds $85.00, his gains will be limited. Although he will realize a substantial benefit from the increase in the value of the stock—from $30.00 at the time he originally made the purchase to $85.00 at the expiration date of the options contract—he will have to sell his stock and will not benefit from any further increase in the value of this investment.

Thus, the protective collar is most appropriate for investors who are long on a stock, bullish on its prospects in the long-term, but concerned about the effects of short-term losses resulting from volatility in the market.

Long Straddle

This strategy is used by investors who want to profit from market volatility as a result of activity on the part of the Federal Reserve Bank, major political events or other significant news reports, or the release of corporate earnings statements. Often, such events can have a dramatic impact on the direction of certain stocks or indexes and can represent an opportunity for investors who want to profit from these changes.

The long straddle is designed specifically to help options traders address the uncertainty inherent in these investment opportunities. Although investors may recognize that significant changes in the stock price of any given security may be imminent, they may be unsure whether that stock price will rise or fall. In such situations, the long straddle can be an effective strategy.

To use this strategy, an investor must first identify the target asset. Next, the trader purchases two options contracts that control the underlying asset—a call option and a put option. Both options contracts should have the same strike price and the same expiration date. In addition, the strike price should be as close as possible to the current market value of the underlying asset. The goal of this strategy is to provide the investor with the opportunity to profit from significant fluctuations in the price of the underlying asset, regardless of whether the share price increases or decreases.

The cost of this strategy is the total cost of buying both options. The payoff comes when the stock either increases or decreases. If the share price rises above the strike price by the expiration, the investor can realize profits by exercising the put option; if the share price falls beneath the strike price, the investor can realize profit by exercising the call option.

Profits will be limited by two concerns. First, the cost of purchasing both options contracts will have to be deducted from any gross profit realized on the price change. Second, depending on the cost of the options contract, the change in share price will have to be great enough to compensate for the expense of setting up the strategy.

Long Strangle

The long strangle is similar to the long straddle and is used in similar situations—for investors who want to capitalize on what they believe is an imminent, significant shift in the value of an underlying asset.

As with the long straddle, an investor using this strategy will purchase both a call option and put option on the same underlying asset, both with the same expiration date. The key difference is that the strike price of each option will be "out of the money." The strike price of the call option will be higher than the current trading value of the underlying asset; the strike price of the put option will be lower than the current trading value of the underlying asset. At the expiration date, if the value of the underlying asset increases significantly enough, the put option will expire and the investor will profit by exercising the call option to purchase assets below market value; if the value of the underlying asset decreases significantly enough, the call option will expire, and the investor can profit by exercising the put option by selling the underlying asset above market value.

Profits will always be reduced by the total cost of the premiums paid to purchase the options contracts. If the value of the share price does not increase to more than the strike price of the call option or less than the strike price of the put option, the investor will lose the entire cost of both options contracts. In addition, if the change in either direction is not significant enough, the investor may be able to recoup some of the costs for purchasing the options contracts, but not enough to generate a profit from using the strategy.

Long Call Butterfly Spread

This options strategy is used by investors who want to profit from underlying assets that they believe will not change significantly in value. To create a long call butterfly spread, the investor will use a bull spread and a bear spread simultaneously. After identifying the stock on which the trader wishes to exercise this option strategy, he will sell two at-the-money call options (two call options, each with strike prices equal to the current trading value of the underlying asset), buy one call option with a lower strike price, and buy another call option with a higher strike price. All of the options will have the same expiration date.

At the expiration date, if the price of the underlying stock remains the same, the investor profits by exercising the call option with the lower strike price. The profit would be the difference between the at-the-money call option and the lower strike price, less the cost of premiums to enter the strategy.

Iron Condor

Like the butterfly spread, the iron condor combines two different strategies—in this case, a bull put spread and a bear call spread. An investor using an iron condor strategy hopes that the underlying asset will not change significantly in value. The profit an investor realizes by using this strategy results entirely from the proceeds of the options contracts themselves.

To implement an iron condor, an investor must first identify the asset on which he wishes to use this strategy. Once he has identified the current market value of the underlying stock, he buys an out-of-the-money put option with a strike price below the current trading value; sells an out-of-the-money or at-the-money put with a strike price closer to or equal to the current trading price; sells a call option with a strike price equal to or slightly above the current trading value; and buys an out-of-the-money call option with a strike price higher than the call option he just sold. The two options the investor has sold are closer to the current trading price of the underlying stock; the two options the investor has bought are at-the-money. Thus, because the out-of-the-money options have lower premiums, the transaction results in a net credit to the trader's brokerage account. At expiration, if the trading price of the underlying stock remains relatively unchanged, all of the options contracts will expire worthless, and the investor will keep the proceeds earned from setting up the strategy.

8

DO'S AND DON'TS

Finally, while all the information in this book should prepare you to enter the world of options trading with some degree of confidence, nothing can really prepare you for live trading. Every situation will be different and may require any one of the strategies we have discussed in this book or some combination of them. Although no one can possibly prepare any options trader for every conceivable transaction, event, or opportunity. Success in this field will come with continued application of the methods, strategies, and knowledge you have gained from this book, and that you will continue to learn as you successfully complete transactions with other investors. However, regardless of the specifics of any given options trade, there are some general "rules of the road" that most traders play by. This chapter includes what we consider to be the most important do's and don'ts of options trading. As you begin your career in this exciting field, we hope not only that you put these strategies work for you but also that you begin formulating your own compilation of road-tested options trading secrets.

What Every Investor Should Do

Understand Market Basics

In the modern world, investment has been made accessible to the average person. Most employers who offer retirement savings plans often sponsor an education day, so employees can gain some familiarity with the types of retirement plans and options that are available to them. In addition, with the proliferation of cable news networks, specialized programming, the internet, and social media, there is no shortage of information widely available to virtually anyone, anywhere.

Especially in the information age, knowledge is power. Before you jump right into trading on the options market, take some time to familiarize yourself with the basics of market dynamics. Options traders use a language that is unique to their niche in the investment world, and many outsiders may be completely perplexed and unable to understand much of what they say. In addition, the ability to tolerate a certain amount of financial risk is an inseparable component of successful investing. Thus, by understanding not only the terminology of the options market but also the fundamental dynamics of the stock market in general, investors can exponentially increase their chances of assembling a profitable career in options trading.

Approach Every Trade with a Strategy

As a beginning options trader, you are familiar with the basic tools of financial planning. You may use professional accounting software for your home and business expenses. At the very least, you probably use a spreadsheet to complete monthly and annual budgeting. Filing taxes every year has given you additional exposure to many of the more technical aspects of financial management. All of this experience acts an excellent foundation for formulating a sound investment strategy.

Chapters 3 and 5 of this book provide detailed information about some of the considerations necessary to formulating an overall investment strategy. If you have not already completed the preparatory steps in those two chapters, be sure to take some time to write out your overall financial goals before you even consider opening an options trading account. Once you have completed the heavy lifting, you will be able to approach each individual options trade with the kind of focus that is necessary for long-term success.

Finally, successful options trading requires that you approach each trade with an equal amount of diligence and planning. Before buying or selling any options contracts, make sure you understand exactly what your goal is for that particular trade. Make sure you have researched the underlying asset and understand current market conditions. Be sure about the strike price and the expiration date. Finally, make sure you have considered all the options strategies available to you. Review the specific strategies outlined in Chapter 7, and don't be afraid to do your own research.

Remember—the market is live. Once you complete an opening transaction, there's no going back. Before you purchase an options contract, ask yourself three important questions:

1. Why should I engage in an options trade on this asset?
2. What do I hope to achieve?
3. What strategy will help me achieve that goal?

If you cannot answer these questions in simple and straightforward language, take some time to formulate a strategy before moving forward. You'll thank yourself later, and so will your fellow traders.

Always Have an Exit Plan

Picking a stock, formulating an options strategy to generate income from the stock's performance, and then contacting your broker to initiate an opening transaction is a good beginning. But this plan is not a complete strategy. The most important part of any options strategy is not how to get in—it's how to get out.

The payoff of an options strategy may result from buying the underlying stock at below market value, from accepting a cash settlement deposit for a put option on stock with declining value, or even from profiting from an increase in the cost of the options premium by selling the contract before it expires.

However you believe the asset you have identified may provide you with an opportunity to construct a profitable options trading strategy, conjecture and hope should not be part of that strategy. Before you complete an opening transaction, make sure you are very clear about your specific goal for entering the contract. After you complete the opening transaction, you will be faced with one of three possible outcomes:

1. The market and the target stocks moved in the direction you predicted.
2. The market or the target stocks move in a direction you did not predict, resulting in unexpected losses.
3. The market or the target stocks move in a direction you did not predict, resulting in unexpected gains.

Similarly, you should have three responses ready for each of these developments:

1. If you are faced with the first result, you should have an exit strategy already prepared. Whatever else is happening around you, as long as your assets are on the right track, do not deviate from your plan.
2. If there are unexpected changes that are not favorable to your position on the underlying

asset, what plan did you formulate to exit the contract so you can minimize your losses?

3. If there are unexpected changes that are favorable to your position on the underlying asset, what plan did you formulate to exit the contract so you can capitalize on these gains?

No matter what happens, make sure you can answer all 3 questions before you enter an options contract. Then, once you have laid the groundwork for a successful options trade, stick with your plan, even if you think you could make a few more dollars by improvising.

Adapt Your Strategy to Market Conditions

Once you're up and running in the world of professional options trading, you will gain confidence as you see your efforts pay off in returns to your options account. As you move from a Level 1 trading account to a Level 2 trading account, you will likely develop a preference for a certain type of options trades— maybe covered calls or married puts. Familiarity with the language and mechanics of the options trading profession is definitely something that will work in your favor. However, it is important to remember that as you move up the ladder, you will gain access to a wider array of trading tools and strategies. As you gain knowledge and experience, remember that no matter how comfortable you have become with a select number of options trading strategies, there will always be additional aspects of nuance that can enhance your skill as a trader and increase the profitability of your efforts. The key to ensuring success is not just in choosing the best strategy in relation to the performance of the underlying asset. You must also consider the overall market conditions and whether those conditions may have an effect on the future performance of that asset. Although one strategy may have worked in the past under similar conditions, considering changes in current conditions will help you adjust your strategy to ensure you continue to build on your past success.

Play by the Rules

As an options trader, you will be in competition with other traders and investors. Much of your success in investing--including making valuable connections in the investment world--will result from your ability to play by the rules. The stock market is a living thing, and the activity of traders has a huge impact on its health and volatility. We are all tempted to be maverick investors who leave a legacy of innovation, but understanding the fundamentals will work in your favor.

Specifically, option prices increase or decrease as a result of changes in share prices and volatility.

So, when share prices increase, call options make money and put options lose money; when share prices decrease, put options make money and call options lose money. Options also move in relation to volatility; when share prices are stable, greater volatility can increase the options pricing. So, when volatility increases, buying options makes money; when volatility decreases, selling options makes money.

Understanding these four basic rules can help you become a better trader.

What Every Investor Should Avoid

Doubling up to Cover Losses

"Doubling up" is a prime example of how an options trader may ignore his original exit strategy if the market or the underlying stocks fail to perform the way he had expected when he originally constructed his strategy.

For example, let's say a trader buys a call option for 100 shares of Company B, with a strike price of $45. At the time he purchased the call option, Company B was trading at $44. The trader expects the share price to rise to $47 before the contract expires. Immediately after the opening transaction, though, the stock price slips to $43.

The premium for a call option with a strike price of $45 is further out-of-the-money now than at opening, In addition, there's still plenty of time before expiration. As a result, to compensate for any potential losses if the stock rises to only $46, the trader may be tempted to "double up" by buying another $45 call option at the reduced premium price.

If this trader were only purchasing stocks, he may have celebrated the unexpected drop in share value and immediately purchased as many additional shares as possible, with a goal of greater long-term return. But options trading works differently. The options trader is focused on short-term returns, and if the stock price fails to put the contract in-the-money by the expiration date, the trader loses on not only one contract, but two.

The smart trader will remember that he created an exit plan for this scenario and will stick with it. Though it may be tempting to purchase an additional call option, he should judge the wisdom of such a purchase by asking himself if he would buy the second call option if he were not already in the middle of a trade. If this is not ordinarily a contract he would enter into--and it isn't, because that was definitely not his strategy in his opening transaction--then market conditions and stock performance that defy expectations are probably the worst reasons for him to change that view.

Instead, he should either stay in his contract to see if the stock eventually rebounds and makes the contract profitable, or sell the contract immediately, cut his losses, and look for another opportunity that makes more sense.

Investing in Illiquid Options

The last time you prepared your company's balance sheet, filed your taxes, or reviewed your investment portfolio, you may have considered your "liquid assets" as part of the calculation of your total assets. Your liquid assets are those assets—such as cars and trucks, office equipment, or real estate—that can quickly be converted into cash by selling them. Assets that have value may not be considered liquid unless you can sell them for cash quickly. Selling assets for cash quickly requires a market, whether you have a garage sale, sell at an auction, or advertise in the media; but it also requires a large enough number of potential buyers that you will not have to wait for the right buyer to come along to pay you the asking price. The more buyers, the more competition, and the greater number of opportunities to make a sale, hence the liquidity of the asset. Obviously, if you are selling an obscure or unique item, regardless of its value, it will be inherently less liquid.

Liquidity in the context of options trading is similar. In order for a stock to be considered liquid, it should be trading at 1,000,000 shares per day. Most "blue chip" stocks—like Microsoft or General Electric--are liquid stocks. Smaller, less well-known companies may not only trade at a lower volume; they made not even trade on a daily basis. Such stocks are considered illiquid.

Like assets and stocks, illiquid options contracts have a relatively small market of buyers and sellers competing for their purchase and sale. All stock traders buy and sell the same stock for any given company; whereas a single stock can give rise to countless options contracts, each with different strike prices and expiration dates. As a result, options are more likely to become illiquid than stocks.

Furthermore, the size of the market for any given options contract may vary from illiquid to liquid even if the stock itself is generally regarded as a liquid stock. A stock is considered to be illiquid if it is trading at less than 1,000,000 shares per day; similarly, you should consider an option to be illiquid if it has an open interest of less than 50 times the number of contracts you will be trading. For example, if you are trading 5 options contracts on XYZ Company, there should be an open interest in options trades for that company of at least 250 contracts.

The primary reasons for avoiding illiquid options markets are cost and return-on-investment. Every time you complete an opening transaction, there will be a buyer and a seller of a contract. That contract will have an ask price (the amount an investor is willing to pay for the contract) and a bid price (the amount for which an investor is willing to sell the contract). But the actual value of the contract lies somewhere between. The more illiquid the option, the greater difference between the ask price and the bid price, and the greater chance you will pay more or receive less for a contract than you should.

Finally, two additional factors can affect the liquidity of an options contract. First, options contracts with strike prices closer to at-the-money and expiration dates in the near-term are generally more liquid. Second, options contracts traded on illiquid stocks are also less likely to be liquid.

Regardless of the reasons for illiquidity, an illiquid options contract will have a greater gap between the bid price and ask price than a similar option in a liquid market. Whether you want to write an option or buy an option, trading illiquid options means losing money on the premium, and the entire reason you are trading options in the first place is to increase your investment income.

Use your time and money wisely and avoid trading in illiquid options.

"Legging in" to Complex Strategies

An options strategy has "legs" if it combines more than one contract. For example, Chapter 7 describes the bear put spread, in which an investor identifies a stock he believes will decline in value. She then buys one put option with a strike price below market value and sells a second put option with an even lower strike price. Both options have the same expiration date but different strike prices. Assuming the stock closes beneath the strike price prior to expiration, the trader receives the cash-settled value of the exercised option and has also reduced the cost of the premium using this strategy. This is the correct way to enter a "spread," which is a range defined by strike prices between which the investor will realize a profit.

Using this scenario, "legging in" means the investor may try to create the spread starting with an opening transaction in which she buys a single put option with a strike price below the current market value. After trading on the contract begins, she watches the market to see when her put option will be in-the-money, then tries to increase her earnings by selling a put option with a strike price below the market value at exercise. This is called "legging in" and involves unnecessary risk—the investor has already realized a profit from the put option she purchased in the opening transaction. Furthermore, if the stock closes at a value below the strike price of the put option she sold, it will expire worthless. In addition, because the premium for the second leg of the spread will decline as a result of time decay, she will receive less for selling the put option after the opening transaction than by creating the spread before trading begins.

Buying Cheap Options

An options contract that is very far out-of-the-money will likely have a comparatively low premium. For example, let's say Company ABC is trading at $30.00 per share. Your broker tells you the share price is likely to increase and that there is a call option on this company with a strike price of $32.00 for a premium of $3.25. You find another call option for the same company with a strike price of $35.00 and a premium of only $1.10. You know the share price is going to increase, and the call option with the lower premium would result in a larger profit, but there's a reason for that--the lower premium results from the fact that the share price is not likely to reach $35.00 by the expiration date. These types of options are traps for beginning traders, so avoid them whenever you can.

Trying to Hit a "Home Run" Every Time

Popular culture portrays Wall Street as a sort of heaven for adrenaline junkies, in which highly skilled traders spend their days chasing down successively bigger, sexier, and more lucrative deals. The only barriers for these imaginary gods of the stock market appear to be failing to out-trade and outperform all their friends and colleagues and thereby missing out on bragging rights at the local pub at the end of the trading day.

A skilled options trader can make huge gains using well-planned strategies. Certainly, this should be a goal for every options trader, but it is a difficult goal to achieve for many reasons. First, the perfect storm of daily skyrocketing corporate share prices hardly ever occurs. Most stocks maintain stability and change very little from day to day, so the textbook conditions for a highly profitable options contract are hard to come by. As a result, if your approach to options trading strategies consists of trying to arrange contracts that guarantee payouts that are not likely to occur, or to approach market analysis from a perspective that a lesser degree of volatility is the exception rather than the rule, you will be missing the considerable opportunities the options trading market presents for disciplined investors.

Markets and indexes may not make dramatic swings very often, and that's probably a good thing. However, markets do consistently move by several points in both directions each day. By studying market behavior, you will have a better grasp of what types of changes are likely to occur and when. Using this knowledge to buy and sell options contracts that conform to sound market fundamentals can help you earn steady weekly returns. Practiced correctly, a well-disciplined approach to options trading can provide any skilled investor with the opportunity to create a source of steady residual income to enhance an existing portfolio.

CONCLUSION

We hope you found this introduction to option trading a valuable resource. Throughout Options Trading: A Beginner's Guide to Highly Profitable Option Trades - Proven Strategies, Trading Tools, Rules, and Money Management we have not only provided a general overview of investment basics, but we have also examined the details of options contracts and how options trading fits in with mainstream investing.

To recap:

- Chapter 1 provides a glossary of terms used both in investing generally and in options trading specifically.
- Chapter 2 maps out the territory of securities trading and where options trading fits in.
- Chapter 3 reviews some of the basic fundamentals of money management and investing.
- Chapter 4 begins a detailed examination of options trading.
- Chapter 5 discusses the pros and cons and benefits and risks of these types of investments.
- Chapter 6 examines in greater detail how to begin investing in options.

- Chapter 7 illustrates some of the specific strategies many options traders use each day.
- Chapter 8 lists some of the do's and don'ts of smart investing.

Reading this book will give you a solid foundation in both the terminology and practice of using stock option contracts to supplement the value of your investment portfolio by hedging against losses caused by market volatility, benefiting from changes in the value of your existing portfolio, and generating an independent income stream that can supplement the value of your returns.

The options market is a well-regulated and exciting place to put your investment knowledge to work for you. Good luck and happy trading!

RESOURCES

7 options trading mistakes beginners can avoid. (n.d.). Retrieved from https://traderhq.com/options-trading-mistakes-beginners-can-avoid/

7 options trading tips for beginners: 3 mistakes to avoid. (2018, November 5). Retrieved from https://www.clydebankmedia.com/blog/finance/investing/options-trading-beginners

Amadeo, K. (2019, February 12). What makes derivatives so dangerous? Retrieved from https://www.thebalance.com/what-are-derivatives-3305833#types-of-financial-derivatives

American Stock Exchange, LLC, Chicago Board Options Exchange, Inc., New York Stock Exchange, Inc., NYSE Arca, Inc., & Philadelphia Stock Exchange, Inc. (1994). *Characteristics and Risks of Standardized Options*. doi: https://www.theocc.com/components/docs/riskstoc.pdf

Angel Broking. (2018, September 4). 7 reasons why options traders get it wrong... Retrieved from https://www.angelbroking.com/blog/7-reasons-why-options-traders-get-it-wrong

Brouster, G. L. (2018, August 20). How to do a market analysis for a business plan. Retrieved from https://www.thebusinessplanshop.com/blog/en/entry/market_analysis_for_business_plan#barriers-to-entry

Chen, J. (2019, April 14). Trendline definition. Retrieved from https://www.investopedia.com/terms/t/trendline.asp

Derivatives - Overview, types, advantages and disadvantages. (n.d.). Retrieved from https://corporatefinanceinstitute.com/resources/knowledge/trading-investing/derivatives/

Downey, L. (2019, September 16). The essential options trading guide. Retrieved from https://www.investopedia.com/options-basics-tutorial-4583012

Downey, L. (2019, September 16). 10 options strategies to know. Retrieved from https://www.investopedia.com/trading/options-strategies/

Five mistakes to avoid when trading options. (n.d.). Retrieved from https://www.optionsplaybook.com/rookies-corner/five-options-trading-mistakes/

Hargrave, M. (2019, September 16). Standard deviation definition. Retrieved from https://www.investopedia.com/terms/s/standarddeviation.asp

Hayes, A. (2019, September 12). Technical analysis definition. Retrieved from https://www.investopedia.com/terms/t/technicalanalysis.asp

Investing in options: A beginner's guide part 4: Greeks. (2017, November 3). Retrieved from https://www.ally.com/do-it-right/investing/investing-in-options-a-beginners-guide-part-4-greeks/

Investor bulletin: An introduction to options. (2015, March 18). Retrieved from https://www.sec.gov/oiea/investor-alerts-bulletins/ib_introductionoptions.html

Investor bulletin: Opening an options account. (2015, March 18). Retrieved from https://www.sec.gov/oiea/investor-alertsbulletins/ib_openingoptionsaccount.html

Nasdaq. (n.d.). Option types: Calls & puts. Retrieved from https://www.nasdaq.com/investing/options-guide/option-types-puts-calls.aspx

Nasdaq. (n.d.). Benefits & risks of options trading. Retrieved from https://www.nasdaq.com/investing/options-guide/options-benefits-risk.aspx

Nasdaq. (n.d.). The Nasdaq options trading guide. Retrieved from https://www.nasdaq.com/investing/options-guide/

Nasdaq. (n.d.). Options defined. Retrieved from https://www.nasdaq.com/investing/options-guide/definition-of-options.aspx

O'Shea, A., O'Shea, A., & Arielle. (2018, November 2). Types of investments. Retrieved from https://www.nerdwallet.com/blog/investing/types-of-investments/

Options are most effective in giving best ROI: Here are some do's & don'ts. (2019, March 14). Retrieved from https://www.quantsapp.com/options-are-most-effective-in-giving-best-roi-here-are-some-dos-donts-2/

Options trading terminology and definitions. (2018, September 6). Retrieved from https://www.ally.com/do-it-right/investing/investing-in-options-a-beginners-guide-part-2-important-terms/

P, K. (n.d.). 10 options trading mistakes every beginner makes. Retrieved from https://www.creditdonkey.com/options-trading-mistakes.html

Palmer, B. (2019, August 25). Mutual funds vs. ETFs: What's the difference? Retrieved from https://www.investopedia.com/ask/answers/09/ mutual-fund-etf.asp

Royal, J. (2017, June 5). 5 simple options trading strategies. Retrieved from https://www.nerdwallet. com/blog/investing/options-trading-strategies/

Royal, J., Yochim, D., & Dayana. (2019, March 1). How to trade options. Retrieved from https:// www.nerdwallet.com/blog/investing/how-to-trade-options/

Schwab.com. (n.d.). The basics of options trading. Retrieved from https://www.schwab.com/active-trader/insights/content/basics-options-trading

Seth, S. (2019, August 27). Use options data to predict stock market direction. Retrieved from https://www. investopedia.com/articles/investing/100115/use-options-data-predict-stock-market-direction.asp

Seth, S. (2019, March 12). Technical analysis strategies for beginners. Retrieved from https://www. investopedia.com/articles/active-trading/102914/ technical-analysis-strategies-beginners.asp

Sraders, A. (2018, November 11). What is options trading? Examples and strategies in 2018. Retrieved from https://www.thestreet.com/investing/what-is-options-trading-14772273

Ticker Tape Editors October 1. (2011, October 1). Naked short dos and don'ts: Pointers for shorting options - Ticker tape. Retrieved from https://tickertape.tdameritrade.com/trading/naked-put-short-options-15035

Top 10 option trading mistakes: Watch how to trade smarter now. (2019, August 20). Retrieved from https://www.ally.com/do-it-right/investing/top-10-option-trading-mistakes/#Trading%20Illiquid%20options

Trading levels at options brokers. (n.d.). Retrieved from http://www.optionstrading.org/getting-started/trading-levels/

What are hard assets and how to invest in them. (n.d.). Retrieved from https://commodityhq.com/investing-ideas/7-hard-asset-investments-you-can-hold-in-your-hand/

What is option trading? 8 things to know before you trade. (2019, August 20). Retrieved from https://www.ally.com/do-it-right/investing/trading-options-for-beginners/

Wolfinger, M. (2019, September 6). Options trading 2019 beginners guide. Retrieved from https://www.stocktrader.com/options-trading/

Yochim, D. (2016, November 21). Options trading terms and definitions. Retrieved from https://www.nerdwallet.com/blog/investing/options-trading-definitions/

www.ingramcontent.com/pod-product-compliance
Lightning Source LLC
Chambersburg PA
CBHW071426210326
41597CB00020B/3669